Independent MEANS

A Canadian Woman's Guide to Pensions and a Secure Financial Future

MONICA TOWNSON

Macmillan Canada
Toronto

Canadian Cataloguing in Publication Data

Townson, Monica, 1932–
Independent means : a Canadian woman's guide to pensions and a secure financial future

Includes index.
ISBN 0–7715–7395–2

1. Women – Canada – Finance, Personal. 2. Retirement income – Canada.
3. Retirement – Canada – Planning. I. Title.

HG179.T69 1997 332.024'042 C97–930326–5

1 2 3 4 5 B–G 01 00 99 98 97

Cover design by Dennis Boyes

Macmillan Canada wishes to thank the Canada Council, the Ontario Ministry of Culture and Communications and the Ontario Arts Council for supporting its publishing program.

This book is available at special discounts for bulk purchases by your group or organization for sales promotions, premiums, fundraising and seminars. For details, contact: Macmillan Canada, Special Sales Department, 29 Birch Avenue, Toronto, ON M4V 1E2. Tel: 416-963-8830.

Macmillan Canada
A Division of Canada Publishing Corporation
Toronto, Ontario, Canada

Printed in Canada

Contents

INTRODUCTION

It was about twenty years ago when it began to dawn on Canadians that women had not been well provided for by the retirement income system. Almost 70% of women on their own who were 65 or older were living in poverty. So it wasn't surprising that when what came to be known as "The Great Pension Debate" kicked off in 1979 the question of how to provide better pensions for women was at the top of the agenda.

At a 1981 national conference on pensions, women and pensions was one of the four topics discussed. It was likely the first time that the subject had come in for such scrutiny. And it was quite a sight as government officials forced all those pension experts—most of whom were men—to consider how the pension system needed to change so women wouldn't have to end their lives in poverty. It helped that the conference was sponsored by what was then called the Department of Health and Welfare and that the minister was Monique Bégin. She had been executive secretary to the 1970 Royal Commission on the Status of Women, and she had a strong personal commitment to women's issues.

As the conference got underway, women's groups made it clear that they felt ill-prepared to make a meaningful contribution to the debate. They wanted more information and an opportunity to discuss pensions for women among themselves so they could make a strong case for reforms that addressed their needs. Bégin decided that Health and Welfare would provide funding for women to organize meetings to discuss pensions and develop recommendations for change.

Meetings were held right across Canada, and I became part of a travelling road show to talk about what needed to be done to give women a decent retirement income. In about 18 months, I travelled from Whitehorse to Charlottetown and just about all points in between. At almost every stop we had audiences of up to 400 women who wanted to talk about pensions and who got into the debate with incredible enthusiasm. It was amazing—and very encouraging—to see how determined women were to make sure they didn't end up in poverty as their mothers and grandmothers so often had.

In the early 1990s, when the Canadian Advisory Council on the Status of Women asked me to take a closer look at the financial future of mid-life women, I jumped at the opportunity. It had been about ten years since the great pension debate. Changes in the pension system intended to help women had been enacted. As well, many more women had gone into the paid workforce. It would be a chance to see how they were doing, how they were managing to save for retirement, and how the prospects for their future financial security had improved.

What I found was pretty depressing. The majority of elderly women on their own were still poor, although now only 56% had low incomes instead of the 70% in 1979. Most women still didn't have a pension plan through their employers. And most weren't saving much for their retirement. Even more worrying was the fact that most women didn't seem to realize what a bleak financial future they faced. With the help of my daughter, Rachel Townson, we spoke to a number of women across Canada. Their stories are told in this book. Their optimism was striking. But the sense of unreality in their comments was disconcerting.

I realized that many women—and probably many men, too—found the pension system difficult to understand. Many women knew that they earned less than men, that they spent a good part of their lives caring for children and other family members without pay, and that they would likely retire earlier and live longer than the men they knew. But they hadn't realized what an impact all of this would have on their financial well-being in their older years.

And so the idea for this book was born. It would explain Canada's complex pension system to women in terms specific to women's lives —and in language accessible to the general reader. And it would give women the information they need to plan for a more secure financial future for themselves.

My thanks go to those women who agreed to be interviewed for the study of Women's Financial Futures and to staff of the Pension Commission of Ontario and the Income Security Programs Branch at Human Resources Development Canada, who read portions of the manuscript and offered invaluable comments. Of course, I alone am responsible for any errors that remain. Thanks are also due to my editor Lily Fong, whose patience and encouragement were so helpful; and to Susan Girvan, at Macmillan Canada, who kept me on track.

Finally, I dedicate this book to my children, Diana, David, Rachel and Michael, to my daughter-in-law Erica and my grandchildren Matthew and Alexandra. I know that their support and encouragement will be there for me as I grow old myself—and that's a comforting thought.

CHAPTER 1

WHY WOMEN'S RETIREMENT NEEDS DIFFER FROM MEN'S

Thousands of words have been written about retirement planning. Pick up any newspaper and you're sure to find something about pensions or Registered Retirement Savings Plans (RRSPs). Tune in to any business show on the radio or on television and you'll be subjected to advice from some retirement planner or financial adviser about how important it is to save for retirement. There's no escaping the message. But has it really sunk in? Do you need to hear it yet again? Or should you just leap into action and do something about it?

Perhaps you need both to hear it again and to do something. But, if you're a woman, it's a fairly safe bet that you haven't heard a retirement planning message that really addresses your needs or concerns. And that's important. If you're going to take effective action to provide a secure retirement for yourself, you need to know what you're up against. That's what this book is about.

This is not just another retirement planning book. Nor is it a book about how to make the most of your RRSP or how to choose the right investments for your plan. Lots of information is already out there about all that. But generic retirement planning advice does not address the particular situations of women because it doesn't take into account the fact that women spend their lives in different ways than men.

Women have different retirement planning needs. Generally, women earn less, retire earlier, and live longer than men. Because of the kinds of jobs women do in the paid work force, we are less likely to be covered by private pension plans. Because of our low earnings, we're also less likely to contribute to RRSPs. Our lifetime patterns of paid and unpaid work are very different from those of men, and that has a big impact on our future financial security and on our retirement planning.

Surprising as it may seem, some women still don't have their own income because most of their adult lives have been spent working without pay in their own homes. If you fit into this category, that means that you're unlikely to have your own pension when you reach that golden age. To paraphrase the old Beatles song, concerns such as "Will he still need you, will he still feed you, when you're 64?" take on added poignancy. Even for women who work outside the home, getting together a decent income for retirement may not be possible without the support of a spouse. This book tells you how to take that into account.

If you've never had a spouse, if you once had one but you're now separated, divorced, or widowed, or if you have a same-sex partner, you'll have different concerns, all of which can affect how you plan for retirement. This book is for you, too.

But let's start at the beginning. Just exactly how are women's retirement needs different? Why a book about retirement for women?

The High Cost of Marriage and Family

One of the most important influences on your future financial security is your marriage—whether that's a formal marriage or a common-law relationship. If you've never been married and you never intend to be, you won't have to worry about this. But when the

1991 population census was taken, only 17 percent of Canadian women aged 25 or older had never been married. That's not to say that some of these women won't take the plunge sooner or later. Marriage, or a long-term relationship with a partner, is something almost all Canadian women will experience at some point in life. You can be sure that marriage or a long-term relationship will have some kind of an impact on your financial situation in old age.

We all know that most Canadian women are now in the paid work force. The "working woman" has become the norm. Of course, the majority of women have always worked. But in Grandmother's day, most women worked in their own homes without pay, looking after the children and doing the housework. The full-time homemaker now seems to have passed into history. Only about 16 percent of two-parent families are supported on the earnings of only one spouse. But for those of you still fulfilling the role of full-time homemaker, providing for retirement has become a question of counting on your mate's pension to support you after he retires, just as his earnings do prior to retirement. There are other ways, too, in which he can provide you with a pension in your own name—some of them with government help.

But what if you're a married woman with your own earnings? You may not be that much better off than your sister who doesn't work outside the home. Believe it or not, marriage has a definite impact on earnings, both for women and men. On average, married men have higher earnings than other men who have never married or who are separated, divorced, or widowed. On the other hand, married women have lower earnings than women who are single, separated, divorced, or widowed. In other words, marriage seems to be a sure-fire way for men to improve their earnings and for women to reduce theirs.

And all that unpaid household work doesn't seem to go away either. If you are a married woman working outside the home, you will likely find that you are still the one to shoulder most of the responsibility for looking after the family and doing the household chores. Differences between women's and men's wages reinforce the pattern. Because your husband or partner earns more than you do, and he probably has a more "responsible" job, you're the one who takes time off if little Amanda is sick or if the baby-sitter doesn't show up. You can't commit to working overtime or to attending meetings in the evenings or on weekends because someone has to look after the kids while your spouse is travelling out of town or working the night shift. That makes you less likely to be considered for promotion—the route to higher earnings. But lower earnings mean you are less able to save for your own retirement.

You may not even be able to consider a full-time job while the children are still little. You may stay out of the paid work force for a few years or you may have to work part-time until the children are old enough to go to school. That means even lower earnings, and your status as a part-time worker may mean you're not covered by the company pension plan either.

Even the Supreme Court of Canada has recognized the problem. Its judgment in the landmark Moge case, handed down in December 1992, pointed out that marriage—whether it's what the courts have called a "traditional" marriage with a breadwinner husband and a homemaker wife, or a "modern" marriage where both husband and wife work outside the home—can have serious economic consequences for women. Mrs. Moge worked full-time as a janitor throughout her marriage. Sixteen years after her divorce, her husband wanted to stop making support payments to her. He said she'd had more than enough time to become financially independent. The Supreme Court disagreed. Madame Justice Beverley McLachlin said, "Even women who have worked outside the home during the marriage may find their career advancement has been permanently reduced by the effort which they have devoted to home and family instead of their jobs, whether the woman be a janitor like Mrs. Moge, or a well-trained professional" (*Moge v. Moge*, [1992] 3 Supreme Court Reports 813, p. 882).

And what's more, said the court, you can't argue that women freely choose whether or not to work outside the home. Social pressures can't be ignored, the court stated. "Mrs. Moge, in keeping with the prevailing social expectations of the time, accepted primary responsibility for the home and the children and confined her extra activities to supplementing family income rather than to getting a better education or to furthering her career. That was the actual domestic arrangement that prevailed," said the court. "What Mrs. Moge might have done in a different arrangement with different social and domestic expectations is irrelevant" (*Moge v. Moge*, [1992] 3 Supreme Court Reports 813, p. 881).

Social and domestic expectations are still playing havoc with women's retirement plans and undermining our financial security in old age. Those expectations are also the main reason more than half of Canada's female senior citizens who are on their own have incomes below the poverty level. That's a wake-up call, if ever there was one, to start doing some serious financial planning now to guarantee yourself a decent income in your golden years.

You may not be a full-time homemaker, or you may not have always worked outside the home, but chances are if you're married—or even if you're now divorced—you spent some time outside the paid work force having children and looking after them. That's going to have an impact on your financial security in retirement, too. The Canada Pension Plan can accommodate brief periods out of the paid work force to raise your children, without reducing your pension. But chances are you lost out on your RRSP contributions while you were at home looking after your kids. You may even have cashed in your RRSP to pay for your maternity leave. But that could have a permanent impact on your retirement nest egg. For example, suppose you have $10,000 in your RRSP and you withdraw $5,000 to finance your maternity leave. Even if you contribute another $5,000 once you return to work, using your regular RRSP contribution limit, to try to make up for the withdrawal, you will have lost the benefit of tax-free compounding of interest on the funds you withdrew. And you may never be able to make up for the interest lost while you were on leave.

If you're lucky enough to have a pension plan from your employer, but you took time out of the work force when your children were young, your pension will probably be lower as a result. However, you may be in the kind of plan that lets you make up for the lost time by making extra contributions to replace those you missed while you were on maternity leave. But that involves extra costs, too, and that may be something you can't afford, especially when you first return to work after having a baby. For example, until recently, if you worked for the federal government, you had to pay triple contributions to the pension plan in the first few years after you came back from child-care leave: your own current contributions, your own contributions missed while you were away, and your employer's contributions missed while you were away. That was tough to do if you were having to pay for child care at the same time.

Even if you took only a couple of years out of the paid work force, chances are you may never be able to catch up to your colleagues who don't have children and have been able to keep right on earning. It's not just the earnings you lose while you're on maternity leave, either. Your absence from the workplace may mean you get passed over for promotion, you lose out on retraining and upgrading opportunities, and you don't accumulate seniority. All that can have a permanent negative impact on your earnings. Some estimates suggest that even labour force interruptions that last as little as two years can have significant long-term costs in terms of lost earnings. Your ability to save for retirement may be permanently affected. It's not a happy thought.

How Marriage Can Improve Your Pension Prospects

Of course, marriage has its good points, especially when it comes to building up a pension. Whether you work outside the home or not, there are ways to share in the pension your spouse has accumulated—even if divorce should intervene to spoil your married bliss. While you may not have much in the way of spare cash to put into your own RRSP, your spouse may use part of his contribution allowance to contribute to a plan in your name. And if he dies, you'll likely be entitled to a surviving spouse pension that's a percentage of his benefit, both from the Canada Pension Plan and from any employer pension plan he may have.

If you get divorced, you're entitled to share in the CPP benefits your spouse has built up during your marriage. And you'll probably also be able to get a share in his company pension. And when you both retire, you can split the CPP benefits between you so you each get a pension in your own names—even if you've never contributed to the plan yourself.

All these provisions are available both to women who don't work outside the home and to those who do. For two-earner couples, this helps the lower-earning spouse, who is almost invariably the wife, and contributes to financial equality between husband and wife. All the provisions apply to both formal marriage and common-law relationships, too. But although some employer pension plans now provide similar benefits for same-sex spouses, the CPP has not yet implemented same-sex benefits. Many people believe it's only a question of time, given the direction in which private pension plans seem to be moving. That could give same-sex partners survivor pensions when one partner dies, and the right to share accumulated benefits when both partners retire.

Keeping Your Economic Autonomy

You may find comfort in being able to count on a spouse to provide you with enough to live on in retirement, but what does this say about your economic autonomy? If you're part of a couple, it's essential that you work with your partner to develop retirement strategies. The way to make sure your interests are protected and your autonomy preserved is to be actively involved in planning, saving, and investing for retirement with your partner. That means equipping yourself with the necessary knowledge and expertise so that you can make sure your needs are taken into account—not just while your partner is around, but after he has gone, too. Asserting your own concerns may not be easy. For instance, many women may feel pressured to sign away their right to receive a pension as a surviving spouse when their husbands die because it means he gets a bigger pension while he's alive. It's great while it lasts, but when he's gone, you may be left with nothing.

And what if you don't have a spouse? Women who have only their own earnings to count on may face tougher challenges. But they can be met. While you may not have the savings and potential pension of a spouse or partner to supplement your own retirement income when you grow old, with careful planning and disciplined saving, you too can provide financial security for yourself in retirement.

Living Longer

One of the key things you need to take into account in thinking about getting older is that women live longer than men. That means we're hit with a kind of multiple whammy. Because our earnings are lower, it's harder to save for retirement. Because family responsibilities—looking after our children earlier in our lives, and perhaps our elderly parents at a later stage—often leave us with fewer years in the work force, we have fewer years in which to save. And because we live longer, we need to accumulate more money than men to provide ourselves with the same kind of pensions. Our retirement income has to last longer. The length of time it has to last may be longer still, when you take into account that women, on average, retire earlier than men.

The life expectancy of both women and men has been increasing. Twenty-five years ago, a woman at age 65 could expect to live another 17½ years, compared with about 13¾ years for a man at the same age. Now, women who get to age 65 can, on average, expect to live another 20 years, while men at age 65 can expect to live close to another 16 years. But when you take into account that women, on average, retire about four or five years earlier than men, you can see that a woman's retirement nest egg has got to last about 25 years, compared with about 16 years or perhaps a bit more for a man's.

That should tell you two important things. First, you'll need a bigger nest egg. How much bigger? To provide an annual income of $40,000 a year for 16 years, you'd need a lump sum of about $450,000. To provide the same annual income for 25 years, you'd need about $630,000. Both numbers assume you'll invest your lump sum and earn an average of 6 percent a year in compound interest. If interest rates are lower, you'll need more; if they're higher, you'll need less.

The second lesson, of course, is that because you're probably going to have a longer retirement period than a man, it's that much more important that your pension income be protected against inflation. Proposals to cut back the indexing of CPP pensions, for instance, would be particularly devastating for women because of the kind of retirement pattern they have.

Another point to keep in mind is that, even if you have a partner now, much of your retirement will be spent on your own. Not only do women live longer than men, but they also generally marry men who are older than they are. About 47 percent of female senior citizens aged 65 or older are widows. At age 75-plus, 64 percent are widows. That's why it's so important to make sure you'll have enough to live on when you have only one income coming in. Remember the old saying: two can live cheaper than one. Living on your own as a single individual is generally more expensive than your half of the costs would be if you can share your living expenses with someone else.

Planning Early and Being Realistic

The key is to start early, get as much information as you can, develop a plan, and stick to it. Above all, be realistic. That may seem obvious, but you'd be surprised how unrealistic most Canadians are when it comes to retirement. Most people think they're going to live well in retirement. In fact, one survey, conducted by benefits consulting firm Towers Perrin in September 1992, found that more than three-quarters of those questioned felt their standard of living in retirement will be the same as, if not better than, it is at present. The trouble is, three-quarters of those same people are doing little or no planning for retirement.

It's difficult to understand why people are so optimistic when they don't even seem to know what kind of financial future they'll face. A few years ago, I spoke to a number of women who were in their forties and fifties to find out how they saw their financial future. They came from all parts of the country and all sorts of backgrounds. Their optimism was certainly striking—in some cases, it was breathtaking.

For example, there was 55-year-old Lise, a divorced woman who had just been laid off from a $70,000-a-year job. She wasn't worried about retirement because she had $30,000 in her RRSP. She was planning to retire at 65. But to provide herself with just $40,000 a year income in retirement—that's only about half of what she was earning before she was laid off—and assuming she wanted to have that annual income for 20 years after age 65, she would have had to save something like $37,000 a year for the next 10 years. This calculation assumes her savings earn interest at an average annual compound rate of 6 percent both before and after retirement. Of course, Lise had never done this calculation. (Chapter 3 will explain how you can do your own calculations.) But she said she didn't have a luxurious lifestyle and, so, didn't expect to have to make any changes when she retired.

Then there was 47-year-old Jennie, who was divorced with five children. She was earning $1,500 a month and belonged to a pension plan at work. With $2,000 in her RRSP, she wasn't worried about retirement either. She felt the Canada Pension Plan would be enough to support her. She hadn't made any other plans for retirement. Jennie wasn't planning to make any lifestyle changes when she retired at age 65, either.

Jennie probably doesn't know that, with her low earnings, if she retired in 1996, the most she could get from the CPP would be about $4,500 a year—and that's not taking into account benefit cuts now being considered by the government. Jennie is probably going to end up having to rely on the new income-tested Seniors Benefit, which, together with her CPP pension, would give her a total annual income in 1996 dollars of about $13,500 at most—well below the poverty level for a single individual living in a city the size of Winnipeg, where Jennie lives now. (These amounts are adjusted each year for inflation so that the purchasing power of the amount Jennie receives when she is 65 will be the same as $13,500 in 1996.) Of course, it's not easy for someone who doesn't earn very much to set aside some of her earnings for retirement. But it can be done. The first step, of course, is being aware that you need to do it.

Fran, a 44-year-old single woman, had also been laid off and was living on Employment Insurance (EI) benefits of $300 a week. She had $50,000 in savings, but she wasn't worried about retirement because she expected to inherit money from her parents. It wasn't clear just how much she might get, nor whether it was guaranteed she'd get it. But Fran wasn't doing anything to plan for her retirement.

Neither was 45-year-old Brenda, a full-time homemaker with two children in their twenties. Brenda was counting on her husband to provide for her. She had no money of her own and her husband handled all the finances. But Brenda didn't even know if her husband had a pension plan. She certainly didn't know if he had made any provision for a pension for her in the event of his death. He was contributing to an RRSP in her name, but she had no idea how much money was in it. In other words, Brenda was totally in the dark about the kind of financial future she faced in her old age. The only worry she expressed was that she and her husband might not have enough money to take a trip or buy a new car after he retired.

Thinking about aging may be particularly difficult for women. In our youth-oriented culture, women's magazines are full of advertising featuring very young women and products to help us stay young and to keep people guessing about our age. As 54-year-old Betty told me, "I never thought I'd get old, so I didn't think about my future." A divorced mother of four grown-up children, Betty was probably the exception that proves the rule among the women I spoke with. She had managed to save $200,000 in her RRSP, she had a pension plan at work, and was looking forward to retiring at 65 with no financial worries.

Betty will probably make it. But there's a powerful message in these women's stories, and that's what this book is about. The only way to guarantee a secure financial future for yourself is to get involved and to start early. Whether you're on your own or with a partner, find out where you stand, think carefully about where you'd like to be when you enter your senior years, and resolve to do something about it now. The younger you are when you start your savings program, the more chance you'll have of attaining a financially secure old age.

We all know it's easier said than done. If you're in your twenties or thirties, planning for your retirement may be the last thing you want to think about right now. As 27-year-old Carmen expressed it, "Nothing could be further from my mind." Her employer, a major national corporation, provides a pension plan for its employees. They don't have to contribute to the plan but they can do so if they wish. Carmen has other priorities. She doesn't know what kind of pension her employer's plan will provide, she is not interested in contributing to the plan herself, nor does she contribute to an RRSP. She hopes to get married one day (and perhaps subconsciously she hopes that some knight in shining armour will provide the financial security she needs), but in the meantime, all her $40,000 annual salary, once she has paid her taxes, goes toward rent, day-to-day living expenses, and paying down her credit card debt. She has also spent money on vacations in the Caribbean, but she has no savings.

Retirement saving is not something 32-year-old Sarah thinks about either—even though her employer is willing to give her a boost to help her save. Working in a retail sales job that pays $11 an hour, Sarah is not married and has no dependents. Her employer set up a group RRSP for workers who had been employed full-time for at least a year. Employees could contribute 5 percent of their monthly pay or $50 a month—whichever they preferred—to an RRSP. Their contributions would be matched dollar for dollar by the employer. But although Sarah is contributing $50 a month to the plan, she sees it more as a way of accumulating savings for other purposes, such as buying a new car, or perhaps setting up her own small desk-top publishing operation. She has already cashed in one RRSP to pay for her car insurance. Now her savings—with the help of her employer—are back up to $1,200, but she doesn't really think about that as the beginning of a retirement nest egg. Yet, if Sarah could keep saving just $50 a month—even without a matching contribution from her employer—and if she could make sure she did not tap into her RRSP savings until she's ready to retire at age 65, she could accumulate a retirement fund of over $150,000 (assuming she earns an average annual compound rate of return on her savings of 10 percent). Of course, she would have much more than this if she increased her monthly contribution as her income rose.

The magic of compound interest means that the earlier you start contributing to a retirement fund, the better off you'll be. In fact, if you start really early and contribute for only a few years, you could have more money when you retire than someone who started later and contributed much longer. The difference is quite startling. For example, suppose at age 20, you manage to save $1,000 a year, and you contribute that amount to your RRSP each year for the next 10 years. At age 30, you stop contributing, but you leave your RRSP intact, until you reach the age of 65. Assuming you earn an average annual rate of return of 10 percent, you'll have about $448,000 in your RRSP by the time you're 65. But suppose you don't start to save until you're 30. From the age of 30 to the age of 65, you contribute $1,000 a year to your RRSP and you earn the same average annual rate of return of 10 percent. By the age of 65, you'll have only $280,000 in your retirement savings fund. Financial planners often use this kind of calculation to illustrate how important it is to start contributing to your RRSP at an early age. But it is also a good example of how women might compensate for the financial impact of their lifetime work patterns. If you can get in just a few years of RRSP contributions before you start having children and incurring other expenses, for example, you can have a good nest egg by the time you retire, even if you can't make any further RRSP contributions for the rest of your life. The key, of course, is to leave your retirement fund alone and to resist the urge to tap into it before you get to retirement.

If retirement is still 40 years down the road for you, the idea of setting $75 or $80 a month aside for your RRSP may seem pointless. But you can see how it would pay off if you take another look at the calculations above. Saving for yourself and starting as early as you can is going to be even more important in the workplace of the twenty-first century. It's a sure bet that if you're now in your twenties or early thirties, you will not work for the same employer all your life. Even if you have a workplace pension plan now, you probably will not always have such a plan. In all probability, you will move to another employer, who may not have a pension plan. It's also highly likely that you'll be doing temporary, part-time, or contract work for a good part of your working life, so you won't have a long-term relationship with any particular employer. You will almost certainly be self-employed at some point and the only way to accumulate savings for retirement will be to do it yourself. Add to all this the fact that government retirement income programs are being downsized and it's clear that you will have to shoulder most of the burden of providing for your own financial security in retirement. It should also be clear that the sooner you get started on your savings plan, the better off you'll be when you reach your golden years.

CHAPTER 2

When are you going to retire?

When are you going to retire? For many women, it's impossible to give a straight answer to that question. Whether you have a paying job or not, there's always the spectre of unpaid work in the home hanging over your head. That's probably why some surveys seem to show that quite a high percentage of female seniors do not consider themselves "retired." Even though they are no longer in the work force, these women are still working in the home. But, of course, that's without pay.

If you have never worked outside the home, you might think that the idea of "retirement" doesn't apply to you. You're probably never going to retire from your lifelong unpaid job—at least not until or unless you reach a stage where someone else will have to care for you. In your situation, "retirement" may happen when your spouse retires from paid employment. That can mean a change of pace or even a more significant change in lifestyle for both of you as a couple.

It wasn't that long ago that a man could expect to go on working for the same employer for most of his working life. Once he turned 65, he got the gold watch and moved gracefully into retirement. For our mothers and grandmothers, life was never that certain or straightforward. Only a woman who never married—and there weren't many of them—could expect to be in the paid work force all her adult life. Even up to the 1950s, women were expected to quit their jobs when they got married. The federal government had a rule that women had to resign when they married. Needless to say, exceptions were made in wartime when women's work was needed to replace the men who were away at war.

In the past 20 to 30 years, more and more women have been working for pay outside the home, but family responsibilities mean that many women don't have a continuous lifetime of paid work. That's probably why it's so difficult for many of us to think of "retiring" as something that will happen on a particular day at a particular time.

But that's increasingly true of men too. The labour market of the 1990s has an ever-expanding number of people doing temporary or contract work, working for themselves as self-employed people without any employees of their own, working for employment agencies, and working part-time. As more and more women and men are involved in these "non-standard" jobs, the way we think of retirement may change completely. Retirement may no longer be a defining moment in time. It's much more likely to be marked by a shifting of gears—the time when you change the kind of work you're doing, perhaps leaving a longer-term, full-time job to set up in business for yourself, or to try a different line of work, one that will give you a bit more time to yourself. You may just want to slow down the pace of your life as you get older by moving from a full-time job in a particular industry to a part-time job in some other line of work.

Even so, that shift in pace is something you need to think about in your retirement plan. If you've planned for it in advance, you may actually achieve the dream of early retirement and freedom at age 55. Switching gears as you get older may also be a fallback position if your savings come up short—too short to let you spend the last 30 years of your life lazing on a beach in the Caribbean. After all, as a woman, at 55, you still have more than a third of your life left to live.

A change of pace can be a much more fulfilling kind of retirement than suddenly quitting work completely because you've reached some arbitrary age.

Many women in the paid work force don't seem to know in advance just when they will retire. One survey by Statistics Canada showed that among people in their late forties and early fifties, 41 percent of women, compared with only 24 percent of men, didn't know when they were going to retire.

Whether you have a paying job or not, it's important to have at least a rough idea of when you plan to retire—however you interpret that term. If your objective is to provide a secure financial future for yourself when you get old, one of the first things you need to know is how long you've got to achieve your objective. If you're in your thirties, for instance, and you plan to retire at the age of 65, but you've managed to save only a few thousand dollars in your RRSP, the situation is not that serious because you've got plenty of time to save more. If you want to retire at 55 and travel the world, you're going to be under more pressure because not only do you have less time to save, but the future lifestyle that you've planned may be more costly than the life you're living now. And if you're now in your late forties and you want to retire at 55, you may have to be very disciplined to accumulate enough money to meet your early retirement objective.

How do you decide on a retirement age? Financial considerations will probably be the main driving force. If you have a pension plan through your employer, the age at which you'll be able to get your pension will be set out in the plan. If most of your retirement income will come from your own RRSP, you'll be able to tap into it at any age, but you must convert your RRSP to some form of income by the time you're 69 at the latest. And if you intend to depend mainly on government programs for your retirement income, you may not be able to get any benefits at all from such programs until you're 60 or even 65.

Somehow, you'll need to take all those considerations into account. Find out where your various sources of retirement income will come from and when they'll be available. Decide on how you can co-ordinate them so that your dreams for a changing lifestyle as you get older can be realized. There are a number of other issues you need to think about.

Family Considerations

Obviously, if you have a spouse or partner, the timing of your retirement is probably going to be a joint decision. Many married women like to retire at the same time as their spouses so that both can enjoy retirement together. As mentioned earlier, because women tend to marry men who are at least a few years older, that means that many women will retire at a younger age than men. The statistics bear that out. And when women who retired before the age of 65 were asked why they retired early, marriage and family responsibilities were two of the main reasons given.

Deciding on a retirement age jointly with your partner is something you can plan for in advance. But whether or not you have a partner, you may also want to consider whether there are other family members you may have to care for in the future. Social services are being cut back at the same time as Canada's population is aging. Governments are shifting much more of the responsibility for caring for the elderly onto families. This has traditionally been women's work, and societal expectations don't seem about to change. If you think you may one day be in the position of having to care for an aging parent or perhaps a family member with disabilities, you should take that into account in your planning, too. Increased family responsibilities as you get older may not necessarily mean you'll have to quit your job completely. But it could mean quitting your full-time job to work part-time if your family responsibilities increase in this way.

Examining that eventuality will give you a more realistic picture of your own future financial situation and help you to plan better for it.

Government Programs

There has been a lot of talk lately about raising the age of retirement. What that generally means is raising the age at which people become eligible for government benefits such as Old Age Security and the Canada Pension Plan. At the moment, government programs are all over the map on this score. You can't get Old Age Security (OAS) until you're 65. And the Guaranteed Income Supplement (GIS)—an income-tested benefit for low-income seniors—is also not available until the age of 65. Both these programs, however, will be rolled into a new income-tested Seniors Benefit, starting in 2001, which will also be payable only at the age of 65. Provincial top-ups for low-income seniors are generally only available to those who are 65 or older, although there are exceptions with some programs in some provinces. These top-ups, of course, are paid only to the lowest-income seniors. With careful planning, though, you won't likely be among them.

You can claim your Canada Pension Plan at any time between the ages of 60 and 70. Another program for older Canadians, the income-tested Spouse's Allowance, can be claimed between the ages of 60 and 64—but you're entitled to it only if you're married to a low-income pensioner or you're widowed. All these programs will be explained in more detail later.

While changes in these programs were announced in the March 1996 federal budget, the Spouse's Allowance program for those aged 60 to 64 will be retained when the new Seniors Benefit, payable at the age of 65, comes into effect in 2001. Effectively, that means that a guaranteed annual income will be available at the age of 60 for low-income, widowed individuals and for those whose spouses are low-income pensioners. But everyone else—including low-income individuals who are single, separated, or divorced, or whose spouses have not yet reached the age of 65—will have to wait until they are 65 to be guaranteed a basic minimum annual income.

A number of women who are single and divorced have been challenging the Spouse's Allowance program through the courts. They're claiming that because the program discriminates on the basis of marital status, it's contrary to the equality provisions of the Charter of Rights. But there's no sign that changes will be made to this program so that low-income people aged 60 to 64 can qualify for benefits, regardless of their marital status. In fact, a previous finance minister actually warned in a budget speech that if such court challenges were successful, the government might consider getting rid of the program rather than extending it to all low-income people aged 60 to 64 because of the increased cost.

In the recent debate about Canada's retirement income system, some people had suggested there should be just one income-tested benefit available at age 60 to all those with incomes below a certain threshold. But that would mean a huge increase in spending by the federal government, which funds these programs, and is almost certainly not in the cards. In fact, government policy seems to be moving in the opposite direction. In the discussion of changes to the Canada Pension Plan, for example, one option being considered is raising the age of eligibility for a full benefit from 65 to 67. The age at which you could claim an early retirement pension, which is lower than the full pension you can now get at 65, would rise from 60 to 62. Some people would go as far as raising the age at which people could claim a full CPP benefit from 65 to 70, phasing it in gradually over a number of years, but there doesn't seem to be much public support for this idea.

Other countries have been raising the age at which people can claim public pension benefits. In the United States, for example, the age of eligibility for social security will go from 65 to 67 over the next few years. Interestingly enough, many other countries, particularly countries in Europe, have public programs that pay pensions to women at 60 and to men at 65. Many of these countries are, however, raising the age of eligibility for women to bring it into line with the age at which men can get benefits.

While raising the age of eligibility for these programs is being driven by the desire to cut costs, policy makers are pointing to improved life expectancy as justification. Credit for choosing 65 as the normal retirement age is given to Count Otto von Bismarck, who was Chancellor of Germany in the late nineteenth century. Economists who have done the calculations say that if 65 was the right age for an American man to retire in 1940, improved life expectancy since then could mean that a man retiring in 1990 ought to do so at the age of 73, and at 75 in 2025. As is usual in these debates, they don't seem to have done the calculations for women. But it's safe to assume that people would not be willing to extend their working life by another 10 years based on this kind of analysis. As retirement incomes have improved and as the standard of living of all Canadians has increased, most people have preferred to take advantage of their improved life expectancy by having more leisure time. That's evident in the fact that almost two-thirds of all Canadians, women and men, now retire before the age of 65.

Clearly, raising the age at which CPP or other government pensions are paid would run counter to what most Canadians prefer. But it's an option that's on the table. And that means taking it into account in your financial planning. You should allow for the possibility that you might not be able to get your CPP pension at 65. Also, make sure that you'll have enough other income in retirement that you won't have to fall back on the income-tested programs such as Spouse's Allowance or the Seniors Benefit.

Mandatory Retirement

What about mandatory retirement? Is there some kind of legislation that would force you to retire, even if you'd like to go on working? This is an important issue for women. Even though most women now retire earlier than men, and most women do so before they hit 65, the freedom to go on working if you want to may be an option you'd want to have in order to protect or improve your retirement income. There's a whole host of reasons why you may need more time than a man to get together enough pension entitlements to secure your financial future, some of which we've already mentioned.

You may not be covered by a pension plan at work, or perhaps you belong to a plan that had discriminatory provisions in the past that may still affect the amount of your pension. If your participation in the paid work force was interrupted for periods of time or if you had periods of part-time work, you may want to work longer to accumulate a better pension.

If you've contributed to the CPP, even if it was only for a few years, you'll get a CPP pension when you retire. But, although the CPP has many important features for women, as will be discussed later, the level of benefits from this plan is pretty low. The most you could get in 1996 was about $8,700 a year. But the average retirement pension women were getting in 1996 was only $3,400 a year. The difference reflects women's low earnings and higher rate of part-time work. Those low earnings, of course, make it difficult to accumulate private retirement savings—another reason you might want to work beyond the normal retirement age. You can start collecting your CPP pension at any time between age 60 and 70, although if you claim it before age 65, you must have substantially ceased working when you start getting your pension. If you claim it after the age of 65, your pension will be increased accordingly.

Perhaps you face financial difficulties as a result of a divorce or the death of a spouse. You may have had to go back to work outside the home when it happened and you may not have had much time to qualify for a pension or save for retirement on your own. And then there's the fact of women's longer life expectancy—another reason you could want to go on earning as long as possible.

New policies and reforms have been introduced to deal with many of the problems women have faced in the past in saving for retirement. Pay equity, for instance, is intended to address the wage gap between women and men; human rights legislation has ended most of the discriminatory provisions of pension plans; and pension reforms have been put into place to deal with some of the disadvantages women faced in the retirement income system. But most of these reforms are very recent. While they will benefit women in the future, they are generally not retroactive. For instance, reforms to the regulations governing employer pension plans were implemented in the late 1980s, so they affect only the part of your employer pension that you accumulated since then. That's why many of these reforms don't do much to help women who are now close to retirement age or who have already retired. If you're in that position, mandatory retirement could have serious consequences.

The good news is that no government legislation, at either the federal or provincial level, prescribes a "retirement age" at which everyone must retire. The problem, though, is that many private pension plans have provisions that require plan members to retire no later than the age of 65. And some employers require employees to retire at or before 65. This requirement has generally come to be known as "mandatory retirement." Needless to say, a provision that says you must retire at a certain age will have the greatest impact on those who have few sources of retirement income or those whose retirement income is likely to be inadequate—in other words, women.

Effectively, mandatory retirement discriminates against people on the basis of age and that's contrary to the Charter of Rights and Freedoms. But the Supreme Court of Canada has ruled that such discrimination is justified because it's "reasonable"—whatever that means. Although it applies equally to both women and men, mandatory retirement is likely to have a greater impact on women than on men because women face a greater risk than men of being poor in old age.

In the 1992 case of a female professor who challenged the mandatory retirement policy of the University of Alberta, the two women justices on the Court had to point out to their male colleagues that mandatory retirement is really a women's issue. In yet another articulate explanation of the situation women face, Madame Justice Claire L'Heureux-Dubé, dissenting from the judgment, wrote that "Women are penalized, in particular, because they tend to have lower paying jobs which are less likely to offer pension coverage, and they often interrupt their careers to raise families. These socio-economic patterns, combined with private and government pension plans which are calculated on years of participation in the work force, in some ways make mandatory retirement at age 65 as much an issue of gender as of age discrimination" (*Dickason v. University of Alberta*, [1992] 2 Supreme Court Reports 1103, p. 1191).

Whether mandatory retirement will eventually be abolished is difficult to predict. Some adjustment may be necessary if the age of eligibility for CPP benefits is raised, because most employer pension plans are "integrated" with the CPP. That means they're based on the assumption that the members of the pension plan will be entitled to a full CPP benefit at the age of 65. If CPP benefits are reduced or the age of eligibility is raised, workers will face a drop in their total retirement benefits, unless employers are willing to bridge the gap. In the meantime, it's important to find out whether your employer pension plan—if you're lucky enough to have one—has a mandatory retirement provision.

If you don't belong to a workplace pension plan, you probably don't need to worry about mandatory retirement. You can go on working as long as you like and use your earnings to supplement your retirement income as you start to receive it. You'll be able to claim your Old Age Security (OAS) or the new Seniors Benefit at 65, as long as your income is low enough for you to qualify; you'll have to close down your RRSP and start withdrawing your funds when you reach 69; and you can postpone claiming your CPP up to the age of 70. If you do this, you'll actually get a higher benefit than you would if you had claimed the CPP retirement pension at 65.

Early Retirement

Everyone has seen those tempting ads that show people relaxing on some tropical island and implying that by the time you get to 55, if you play your cards right, you'll have the "freedom" to enjoy all that sun and sand. But if early retirement is in your sights, you'll have to start planning almost as soon as you start working. Those ads are apparently directed at people in their twenties. In most cases, to have enough money to enjoy a life of leisure by the time you reach age 55 involves socking away money for your retirement at a very early age and making sure you never have to tap into it in an emergency. For most people, that's probably not realistic. We generally have other priorities when we're in our twenties, such as getting an education, buying a house, and having children. As well, in the uncertain times we're now experiencing, we can't be sure we'll never have to tap into our retirement nest egg in an emergency.

Just the same, early retirement seems to be something that most Canadians have in mind. And somewhere around 55 seems to be the most popular age to do it. Statistics Canada, which surveys these things, found that men are more likely than women to have such plans. Early retirement also seems to be popular with the baby boom generation—that is, people born between 1946 and 1965. About 56 percent of men in this age group were planning early retirement, compared with only 40 percent of women.

As you might expect, income and pension prospects are likely to be the main determinants of early retirement plans. The same surveys also showed that the lower their household income, the less likely people were to have concrete retirement plans and to choose early retirement. It goes without saying that having an employer-sponsored pension plan makes early retirement more feasible. More than half of workers with employer pension plans wanted to retire before the age of 65, compared with just over one-third of those without such pensions. Given that the majority of women don't have employer pension plans, and have lower earnings, and face more uncertainty regarding financial security in retirement than men, it's hardly surprising that so many women have no clear idea of the age at which they will retire and that only a minority of women seem to be planning early retirement.

Early Retirement with the Help of the Tax Department

Most employer pension plans allow for early retirement—often at about the age of 55—with a reduced pension. That's something to check for if you have a workplace pension plan. In some cases, you can even take early retirement without a reduction in benefits as long as you meet certain conditions. But private pension plans have to be registered with Revenue Canada for the contributions to be tax-deductible, and government regulations set minimum conditions for early retirement without a reduction in benefits.

Workers in certain prescribed occupations are exempt from the restrictions on early retirement because their jobs involve public safety. These people are allowed to retire early without having to accept a lower pension. The prescribed occupations are firefighter, police officer, corrections officer, air traffic controller, and commercial airline pilot. People in the armed forces are also exempt from the rule.

Interestingly enough, the exempt occupations are all ones in which men predominate. Nurses and flight attendants, who work in female-dominated occupations, have argued that their jobs should be included in the list of occupations for which early retirement with unreduced benefits at 55 is permitted. The National Federation of Nurses Unions, for instance, argued before a parliamentary committee that the high degree of stress in the nursing profession, as well as the heavy mental and physical demands on nurses, raised issues of public health and safety if nurses were required to continue working until the age of 60 to receive full pension benefits. Their efforts were in vain and the list of prescribed occupations remains unchanged.

When it comes right down to it, whether or not you'll have enough money to live on will determine whether your plans for early retirement are feasible. That's why sitting down to do the necessary calculations is so important. That will be discussed in the next chapter.

Phasing into Retirement

Picking a retirement age, of course, does not have to be an all-or-nothing exercise, as mentioned earlier. If your dream of early retirement just isn't feasible financially, one solution is to phase into retirement gradually. There is already talk about adapting the Canada Pension Plan to allow people to do this. Under the current rules, you must have "wholly or substantially" stopped working when you claim your CPP retirement pension unless you're 65 or older when you claim it. You can also claim your CPP pension if your earnings from work are less than the maximum annual CPP retirement pension payable at age 65 for the year you make your claim.

There's nothing to stop you going back to work once you've started getting your CPP pension, but you would not be able to start contributing again and you would not be able to improve your CPP pension by starting to work again.

Some countries, such as Sweden, provide for phased retirement or "partial pension" in their public pension programs. In such situations, people can start claiming part of their pension while they continue to work—perhaps switching from full-time work to a part-time job. It's a way of easing into retirement gradually. And it helps the public pension program, too, because contribution revenue continues to be collected and the plan doesn't have to pay out as much in benefits. We may yet see such a provision in the CPP. But there's an important difference between Sweden and Canada. Sweden's public pension program offers a pension that's worth about 60 percent of an employee's earnings before retirement, up to a maximum. Our CPP gives you only 25 percent of your average pre-retirement earnings up to a maximum.

Phased retirement, if that's what you'd prefer, may take some planning, but it can be done. It's a question of scheduling your retirement income to phase in at the same time as you're phasing out.

The Age at Which Women Retire

When it comes right down to it, most Canadians now retire before the age of 65. Of all those who started getting their CPP retirement pensions in June 1996, 66 percent of women and 59 percent of men had retired before turning 65.

In fact, quite a high percentage of women retire before they are 60. One survey by Statistics Canada in 1989 showed that 22 percent of women surveyed had retired when they were under the age of 55, while another 21 percent had done so between 55 and 59. Only 26 percent of the women surveyed had retired when they were 65 or older. Of course, this survey was looking at the traditional definition of "retirement," that is, quitting the paid work force.

Only 28 percent of the people surveyed—both men and women—had retired because they had reached mandatory retirement age. Health reasons, almost as important in determining retirement age, were cited by more than one in four of those individuals who had retired from paid jobs. The kind of job you have doesn't seem to make much difference to the age at which you'll retire—at least according to this survey. Most people chose their age of retirement based on their own personal choice or preference. For women, marriage or family responsibilities were the two main factors that influenced their choice.

CHAPTER 3

HOW MUCH MONEY WILL YOU NEED?

How much money will you need in retirement? There is no magic dollar figure. Sometimes people ask, "How much does a woman need to live on in retirement?" It's impossible to answer that question because the answer depends on the individual woman. It depends on: how you plan to spend your time in retirement; what kind of income you're used to having; whether you're willing to adjust your lifestyle or standard of living, if necessary, to cope with a lower income; whether or not you have a partner or spouse; and a host of other questions that need to be answered by you before anyone can estimate a dollar figure. Only you yourself can decide how much money you'll need to live on in retirement because only you can make those lifestyle choices that have to be made before anyone can make a dollar estimate.

Thinking about what you want to do when you retire is probably the most important part of planning for your future financial security. Merely having some vague goal such as "travel" or "start a business" or "work as a volunteer" is not good enough. If these really are your goals, you'll need to be much more specific than that, otherwise you may not be able to achieve them.

Where are you going to travel? Will you be on your own or with a companion or partner? (It makes a difference—travelling on your own can be much more expensive than travelling with someone else: when there are two of you, you can split the cost.) What would it cost to travel to the places you'd really like to visit? If you plan to spend extended periods of time in one place or another, what will it cost to live there for months at a time?

What kind of business do you want to start? Have you really researched what sort of financing you would need? Can you afford to take risks with your savings? Saving the capital you need to start a business—if that's what you have really set your heart on—has to be factored into your retirement plan as well.

Even doing volunteer work all day is only feasible if you have enough money to live on without having to work for pay.

Making these kinds of lifestyle choices is not easy. The closer you are to retirement, the clearer you may be on how you would like to spend your time. But, of course, the closer you are to retirement, the less time you have to save the money you need to meet your objective. The good news is that there is all sorts of information, including free planning guides, to help you. Most financial institutions have free retirement planning booklets outlining what you need to consider in some detail. For example, the Royal Bank's booklet called Retirement, which is in the bank's Your Money Matters series, has a planning checklist that goes through the kinds of things you need to think about, such as whether your hobby can earn extra cash for you in retirement, whether you want to live with family members, and whether you want to sell your house and move to a smaller one. Check with your bank, trust company, or credit union to see what it has in the way of free information that you can use as a guide.

If you have a spouse or partner, your plans for the future should also consider what would happen if you end up being left on your own by the time you get to retirement age. Chances are you'll be on your own eventually anyway, as already discussed, so that needs to be taken into account, too. (More detail about how your pension may be affected by divorce or widowhood will be provided later in the book.)

If you're still under the age of 40, all of this may seem very far down the road. But that doesn't mean you can't do some planning now. The best way to go about it, regardless of how old you are now, is to think in terms of replacement income. In other words, how much annual income will you need in your older years to replace the money you now get from your earnings—or from the joint earnings of you and your partner, if you have one?

Your Cost of Living as a Senior

In all probability, you won't need the same income in retirement as you do now. That's because you will no longer have some of the expenses for which you're now shelling out. You won't have the cost of travelling to and from work, for example. You won't have to get dressed up to go to the office, so you probably won't spend as much on clothes. But the idea that your cost of living will be a lot lower when you're a senior is not necessarily true, although it seems to be a popular myth about seniors.

For instance, the claim is often made that once you retire, your mortgage will be paid off and your children will have grown up and left home, so your expenses will drop quite a bit. But these life-changing events generally happen long before you get to retirement age. Take your mortgage, for instance. If you bought your house when you were in your late twenties, let's say, with a 25-year mortgage, it will be paid off by the time you're in your early fifties—before you retire. And even if you're living in a mortgage-free home, you still have the cost of running it. Expenses for heating, insurance, hydro—not to mention property taxes—are not going to go down once you retire. They may even go up. So, you're going to need an income to keep your house going, even if it is mortgage-free, as long as you continue to live in it. There are ways, however, in which you can use your home to support yourself financially as you get older. These will be discussed in more detail later.

If your children were born when you were in your late twenties and early thirties, they will be in their thirties or even forties by the time you retire. Hopefully, they will have left home long before you're in your sixties. Financially, the timing of these major events should allow you to boost the funds you're setting aside for retirement. Once your mortgage is paid off, for example, you can continue to set aside the amount of the mortgage payment each month as a contribution to your retirement fund. But, because events such as paying off the mortgage or children leaving home generally occur a few years before your retirement, they are unlikely to mean you'll face a sharp drop in your cost of living at retirement.

You may have seen reports in the media claiming that low income among seniors is not really as serious as some people think because the kind of expenses seniors face are lower than everyone else's. That kind of thinking is misleading, so don't put too much emphasis on that when you're considering how to provide for your own future financial security.

Some years ago, Statistics Canada did some research to see if there should be a separate cost of living index for seniors. What most people think of as "the cost of living index" is actually the Consumer Price Index (CPI), Canada's main measure of inflation. It is based on a combination, or "basket," of goods and services that the average family might buy. Each month, a survey measures how the cost of items in that typical basket of goods and services has increased. The result is then used to estimate the CPI for the month. If seniors don't buy the same kind of package as the rest of the population, then maybe seniors don't face the same kind of inflation rate as younger Canadians. But the survey showed there was very little difference between seniors and younger Canadians in the goods and services they buy. In other words, your cost of living as a senior is unlikely to be that different from your cost of living before retirement.

Still, you may be somewhat better off financially once you stop working. For example, you'll no longer be contributing to the Employment Insurance (EI) program or to the CPP. For example, the average earnings of a woman who worked full-time for a full year in 1994 (the latest year for which these data are available) were $28,400. If you were earning that salary in 1996, you were paying roughly $1,600 a year in contributions to these two programs alone. And if you were contributing to a workplace pension plan, that contribution will no longer be taken off your income. In other words, because of these financial savings once you stop working, your total income, before taxes, could drop quite a bit, without having any impact on the amount of disposable income you have available for day-to-day living expenses.

Then there are the special tax credits available to seniors: the age credit for those aged 65 and over, whose incomes are below a certain threshold; and the pension income credit for the first $1,000 of pension income, not counting OAS and CPP. These tax credits also add to your disposable income, but keep in mind that they are about to be eliminated when the new income-tested Seniors Benefit is implemented in 2001.

As a senior, you may also be able to benefit from: a government-sponsored free drug plan, depending on the province in which you live; access to subsidized housing; and other special preferences such as cheaper admissions (to parks, museums, and art galleries), cheaper tickets on public transportation, and no-charge bank accounts. Just how much difference all this will make to your living costs will depend on how much you use these services. But keep in mind that seniors are now being asked to pay some of the cost of their prescription drugs and long-term care. As well, as governments cut back their spending on social services and income support programs, there seems to have been a disturbing increase in anti-senior rhetoric in the media. In the U.S., it has been referred to as the "kids versus canes" debate. And it seems to be based on a feeling that seniors have never had it so good and that maybe they should be asked to "sacrifice more" to help young people. If these trends continue, we may see the gradual disappearance of many of the financial breaks seniors now get.

The moral of the story is that you shouldn't count on getting any of these perks as you move into your senior years. In any case, the objective of retirement planning is to make sure you have adequate financial support in your old age so that you are not forced to rely on subsidized housing, social assistance, or any other programs designed to help those who have not been able to provide for themselves. In an era of continuing government restraint, such programs are always vulnerable. And while seniors' discounts can be an added bonus, it's better to assume they won't necessarily always be there. Make sure you don't have to count on them to survive during your older years.

Estimating a Replacement Income

How are you going to figure this all out? One way of calculating your replacement income is to use the rule of thumb that many financial planners use. They say that to maintain your current standard of living in retirement, you need anywhere from 60 to about 80 percent of what you had coming in prior to retirement. These "replacement ratios" are based on your total income before taxes and they take into account the kind of savings that were discussed earlier, such as no longer having to make EI and CPP contributions and mortgage payments, and the availability of special seniors discounts and savings.

Just exactly where in that 60-to-80-percent range you might fit depends on your own individual circumstances. If you own your home mortgage-free, for example, you may fall at the lower end of the range, compared with someone who is renting and may face rent increases throughout her retirement. According to some estimates, a mortgage-free home as opposed to a rental may represent a saving equivalent to as much as 20 percent of your pre-retirement income.

If you plan a complete change in your lifestyle, you may be at the higher end of the range. For instance, if you plan to travel extensively, the higher cost of your travel for pleasure may more than offset what you save by not having to travel to work any more. You'll need to consider all of the possibilities and come up with a replacement ratio that fits your particular circumstances.

There's another important consideration that's especially relevant to women, whose earnings generally average so much lower than those of men. If your income before retirement was so low that you were only just getting by, you're going to need a much higher percentage of your pre-retirement earnings to have a decent standard of living in retirement. For instance, if your pre-retirement income was $28,000 a year, 60 percent of that would give you only $16,800 in retirement. That would be a poverty-level income for a single individual living in a big city. At this earnings level, you may need to think about a replacement ratio of 80 percent or even higher.

How could you possibly meet such an objective? The answer may be that you can't, but you can perhaps think about ways in which you can supplement your pension income by continuing to earn as you get older—maybe through a part-time job or some other way in which you can earn extra money. Those strategies will be discussed in the last two chapters of this book.

It goes without saying that if you're planning your future financial security with a spouse or partner, you'll need to come up with a joint replacement ratio for your joint incomes.

Options for Figuring It Out

Let's assume, for the sake of argument, that you settle on a replacement ratio of 70 percent. How will you meet that target? And how does it translate into the dollar amounts you'll need to save each year to meet your goal? Working with 70 percent of your current salary, you will be able to estimate the annual income you'd like to have in retirement. But you'll also have to take into account the number of years you might want to have that annual income coming in—in other words, how long you expect to live in retirement. For instance, suppose that at 65, you would like to start getting an income equivalent to $40,000 a year in today's dollars for the following 20 years. Your calculations might tell you that you would have to have a lump sum of about $463,000—assuming you start out with this amount at 65 and it earns an average 8 percent compound interest a year, while providing you with your annual income. You'll then have to calculate how much you'll have to save each year to accumulate that amount of money by the time you are 65, taking into account inflation, potential interest earned on your money as you save it, the number of years you have left until your planned retirement age, and so on.

You can do some fairly simple calculations yourself with the help of an ordinary calculator. You can also make use of a computer program, which will figure it out for you, once you've fed in some basic information about yourself. You can go to a financial institution, which can help you through the process, perhaps even without charging a fee. Or you can pay a professional financial planner to do a tailor-made projection for you. The first step, however, is to estimate how much of your replacement income needs are already taken care of by government programs such as OAS and CPP, by your workplace pension if you have one, and by the amount you've saved in your RRSP so far.

Where Will the Money Come From?

The income you'll need to replace your pre-retirement earnings can come from a variety of sources, including government programs, your company pension plan, your RRSP, your other investments, your home, self-employment, or perhaps a continuing part-time or even full-time job.

Today's seniors still get quite a high percentage of their income from government programs such as the OAS and CPP, as well as the Guaranteed Income Supplement (GIS), which goes only to low-income seniors. Women aged 65 or older are much more likely than men in the same age group to rely mainly on transfer payments from these government programs for retirement income. The table below shows where today's seniors get their income.

The "investment income" referred to in the table includes: interest on deposits, such as bank accounts; bond interest and interest on savings certificates; dividends; capital gains; and income from other investments, such as rental income and cash dividends from life insurance policies. "Government transfer payments" include: OAS and GIS; CPP or QPP benefits; Employment Insurance benefits; social assistance and other government income such as veterans' pensions, government training allowances, and worker's compensation. The category of "other money income" includes: pensions from workplace pension plans; income from RRSPs and RRIFs; annuity income; income from scholarships; royalties; and alimony payments.

What you'll need to do is decide where you'll fit into the picture. Will you have to rely mainly on government programs for your retirement income needs? And how much of your income needs can be met from these programs? You can find out the actual dollar amounts you can get from the OAS and CPP today, but there's no way of knowing exactly what benefits those programs will be paying when you retire. Besides, the programs may have changed by then.

Seniors' Sources of Income, 1993

	Women %	Men %
Wages and salaries	3.6	7.6
Net income from self-employment	0.7	3.6
Investment income	19.0	13.3
Government transfer payments	61.5	46.8
Other income	15.2	28.7
Total	100.0	100.0
Total average income	$14,845	$23,366

Source: Statistics Canada, "Survey of Consumer Finances."

There are a couple of ways in which you can approach this. One is to do what many financial planners suggest—assume you won't get anything at all from government programs and that you'll have to provide for your retirement income needs entirely by yourself through a pension plan at work and RRSPs or investments. But that's probably not a very realistic option for most women, who are not likely to belong to a workplace pension plan and probably don't have much spare cash to contribute the maximum amount allowed to an RRSP. If you're in that position, you will have to count on getting at least a basic amount from government programs.

A more realistic approach is to work from a percentage basis. Start by figuring out what percentage of your replacement income needs might be met from OAS and CPP and from your workplace pension. Then see what's left for you to save for yourself.

How Government Programs Meet Your Replacement Income Goals

Even though you won't know the exact dollar amounts that might be paid from the government programs in the future, it is possible to estimate roughly what percentage of your pre-retirement income you'll get from these programs. For example, if you've been in the paid work force most of your adult life, with perhaps brief periods at home when you had children, your CPP pension will be 25 percent of your average annual earnings, up to a maximum equivalent to the average wage.

Until recently, you could also count on getting part of your retirement income needs from Old Age Security. For some years now, OAS benefits have been roughly equivalent to about 14 percent of the average wage. So, if your annual earnings are at the average for all workers, which in 1996 was about $35,400, you could count on getting approximately 39 percent (25% + 14%) of your pre-retirement earnings from CPP and OAS combined. To meet a replacement ratio of 70 percent, then, you would need to generate 31 percent (70% – 39%) of your pre-retirement earnings from your own savings or workplace pension plan; in other words, 31 percent of $35,400 means that you need to generate an income of just under $11,000 a year from these sources.

However, because OAS is a flat-rate benefit and the amount is not related to earnings, it represents more than 14 percent of pre-retirement earnings for someone whose earnings are below average. For instance, let's suppose you're making only $25,000. The full OAS benefit, which in 1996 was about $4,800 a year, would be equivalent to about 19 percent of your pre-retirement earnings. With the CPP at 25 percent of your average earnings, you would get 44 percent (25% + 19%) of your pre-retirement earnings from CPP and OAS, and you would need to generate an additional income of only 26 percent (70% – 44%) of your pre-retirement earnings, which works out to $6,500 a year, to give you a retirement income of 70 percent of your pre-retirement earnings of $25,000.

But the government has already announced major changes to the OAS program. It will no longer be a flat-rate benefit, payable to everyone at the age of 65, regardless of whether the individual has been in the paid work force and regardless of any other income the individual may have. Starting in 2001, OAS will be converted to a welfare program, available only to those people whose incomes are low enough to qualify. It will be an income-tested benefit and the income test will be based on family income. That means married women will no longer be able to qualify for a benefit in their own right. Because men's incomes are generally higher, both before and after retirement, a married woman's right to the new Seniors Benefit, effectively, will depend on the spouse's income. Whether you're married or not, these changes mean you can no longer count on OAS to replace a portion of your pre-retirement income—unless you're already in your sixties, in which case you'll have the option of remaining under the old rules.

To make matters worse, the government is also considering reducing the replacement rate of the CPP pension from the current 25 to 22.5 percent. All of this makes planning for your future financial security a much more uncertain exercise. You will want to allow for these changes in your retirement income planning—perhaps by assuming that your CPP pension will replace only 20 percent of your pre-retirement earnings if you're earning at or below the average wage. If you're earning more than the average wage, of course, your CPP pension will be even lower as a proportion of your pre-retirement earnings. For example, the maximum CPP retirement pension in 1996 was about $8,700, which is only about 19 percent of pre-retirement earnings for someone earning $45,000 a year.

Income from Your Workplace Pension

If you expect to get a pension through your employment, you'll need to factor that into the equation, too. Just exactly what benefit you'll get from your workplace pension may be difficult to determine, as will be explained in Chapter 5. If you have a top-notch pension plan, as you might if you work for the federal government or for a large corporation in the private sector, for example, you may be entitled to a pension that's equivalent to 2 percent of your average annual earnings over your six best earnings years for each year of service up to a maximum of 35 years. (This is the benefit formula for the federal public service pension plan.) If you work for that employer for 35 years, your pension won't necessarily be 70 percent of your salary just before you retire, but it will be 70 percent of what you were making over the six best years of earnings. For example, if your average annual earnings over your six best earnings years are $50,000, you would take 2 percent of that, which is $1,000, and multiply it by 35 years, which gives you a pension of $35,000 a year when you retire. This $35,000 would represent 70 percent of your average salary based on your six best years of earnings. This pension, together with what you'll get from the government programs, will probably be enough to meet your replacement income goal. Any additional savings you can manage to set aside will improve your well-being in retirement or help you meet other objectives such as travelling around the world or lounging on a tropical island for months at a time.

But not many women are likely to be in this fortunate position. Most women don't have a workplace pension at all. And even those who do may not have one that's this generous.

Estimating Your Retirement Savings Goal

Unless you're lucky enough to belong to a good workplace pension plan, you will probably have to provide most of your retirement income needs yourself from your own savings. But how much will you have to save to support the kind of lifestyle you'd like to have in retirement? This calculation is the key to your future financial security. You can approach it in several different ways.

Do It Yourself the Old-Fashioned Way

Many financial institutions have free workbooks that take you through the various steps needed to calculate your retirement savings goal. One of the best was put out by Scotiabank. This workbook is no longer printed, because the bank now offers a more sophisticated retirement planning model that you can see on the Internet (www.scotiabank.ca), which is described later. However, the formula below, reproduced with permission, is still useful and still usable.

Scotiabank's Seven-Step Calculation

How do you know if your current RRSP savings and future contribution amounts will be enough to fund your desired retirement lifestyle? By following the seven easy steps outlined below, you can get an answer. All you need is a pencil and a calculator.

To begin, you have to determine how much RRSP savings you will need to accumulate by the time you plan to retire. Once you have this figure, you can then work backwards to determine how much you need to save each year in order to attain this goal.

Part I: Determine Your RRSP Accumulation Goal

Step #1: *How much retirement income do you want?*
If you were retired right now, would you need the same annual income you are currently earning? Keep in mind that you probably won't have a mortgage or any other major debts, although you may have new expenses, depending on your hobbies or interests. The general rule of thumb is that you'll need 60 to 80 percent of your pre-retirement annual income.

Write down the annual income you would like to receive during your retirement, based on what you are earning today, and multiply it by the appropriate Inflation Factor. Choose the Inflation Factor that corresponds to the number of years in which you plan to retire. You can do this separately for you and your spouse or you can do a combined amount.

INFLATION FACTORS

Number of years until you plan to retire	2% compound annual inflation rate
5 years	1.104
10 years	1.219
15 years	1.346
20 years	1.486
25 years	1.641
30 years	1.811
35 years	2.000

Annual Retirement Income that you want:

$______	x	______	=	$______
Annual Income		Inflation Factor		Annual Retirement Income

Step #2: *How much of this income will come from your RRSP savings?* Retirement income usually comes from the following sources: government pensions (CPP/QPP), Old Age Security (OAS), company pensions, income from investments, income earned usually through part-time jobs, and income from RRSP savings. In 1990, pensioners claimed 44 percent of their retirement income from government sources (CPP/QPP/OAS) and 35 percent from company pensions.

For more information on government retirement programs, find the Government of Canada section in the blue pages of your phone book and look under Human Resources Development—Income Security Programs (formerly Health and Welfare Canada).

Retirement income from RRSP savings will generally range from 0 to 50 percent of your total retirement income. To determine the percentage of your retirement income that will come from your RRSP savings, multiply your desired annual retirement income (from Step #1) by the percentage that fits your situation. We suggest 10 to 25 percent if you have a company pension and 40 to 50 percent if you don't have a pension plan. Or, use a higher percentage if you're skeptical about the future availability of government pensions.

Desired Annual Income from RRSP Savings:

$__________	x	__________	=	$__________
Annual Retirement Income		% from RRSP		Desired Income from RRSP

Step #3: *Calculate your RRSP Accumulation Goal*
How many years do you want to receive this income and what do you estimate your investment return will be over these years? Of course, no one knows exactly, but you need an estimate to do your projection. Use the chart below to obtain the Retirement Projection Factor that corresponds to the approximate number of years you want to receive an income from your RRSP savings and your estimated investment return for these years. For instance, if you want the income for 20 years and estimate an 8 percent return on your RRSP savings, the corresponding Retirement Projection Factor is 11.580.

Multiply your desired income from your RRSP savings (Step #2) by your Retirement Projection Factor.

This is your **RRSP Accumulation Goal**—the amount you've determined you need to accumulate in your RRSP. If the assumptions you made hold true, this amount will allow you to draw the annual income you want from your RRSP savings (which increases by 2 percent each year because we factored a 2 percent inflation rate into the Retirement Projection Factors) for the number of years you indicated.

RETIREMENT PROJECTION FACTORS

Number of years income is needed	Compound annual investment return 4%	6%	8%	10%
5 years	4.719	4.462	4.226	4.009
10 years	9.001	8.143	7.401	6.758
15 years	12.887	11.180	9.787	8.642
20 years	16.413	13.685	11.580	9.934
25 years	19.614	15.752	12.928	10.819
30 years	22.518	17.458	13.940	11.426
35 years	25.153	18.865	14.701	11.843

Your RRSP Accumulation Goal:

$________ × ________ = $________

Desired Income from RRSP × Retirement Projection Factor = RRSP Accumulation Goal

By following the next 4 steps, you'll get the amount you need to contribute annually in order to reach this goal.

Part II: Determine Your Required Savings Pattern

Step #4: *How much do you currently have in your RRSP?*
If you already have an RRSP, then you're on your way to achieving your RRSP Accumulation Goal. Write down how much you currently have invested in your RRSP(s).

Amount you currently have in your RRSP(s) is:

$________

Step #5: *How much will your current RRSP(s) be worth at retirement?* Project the value of your current savings into the future. Use the chart below and obtain the Future Value Factor that corresponds to the approximate number of years until you plan to retire and your estimated compound annual investment return during these years. For instance, if you plan to retire in 25 years and during those years you estimate your RRSP savings will earn 8 percent, your Future Value Factor is 6.848.

FUTURE VALUE FACTORS

Number of years until you plan to retire	Compound annual investment return			
	4%	6%	8%	10%
5 years	1.217	1.338	1.469	1.611
10 years	1.480	1.791	2.159	2.594
15 years	1.801	2.397	3.172	4.177
20 years	2.191	3.207	4.661	6.272
25 years	2.666	4.292	6.848	10.834
30 years	3.243	5.743	10.062	17.449
35 years	3.946	7.686	14.785	28.102

Multiply the amount you currently have in RRSPs (Step #4) by your Future Value Factor. This is the projected value of your current RRSPs by the time you plan to retire.

Future Value of your Current RRSP(s) is:

$__________	×	__________	=	$__________
Current Value		Future Value Factor		Future Value of Your RRSP(s)

Step #6: *What is your Net RRSP Accumulation Goal?*

If you already have money invested in RRSPs, your RRSP Accumulation Goal will be reduced by the future value of your current RRSP savings. To obtain your Net RRSP Accumulation Goal, subtract the future value of your current RRSP savings (Step #5) from your RRSP Accumulation Goal (Step #3).

Your Net RRSP Accumulation Goal is:

$__________	–	__________	=	$__________
RRSP Accumulation Goal (from Step 3)		Future Value of your RRSP(s) (from Step 5)		Net RRSP Accumulation Goal

This is your **Net RRSP Accumulation Goal**.

Step #7: *How much do you need to save each year to reach your goal?*

Take your Net RRSP Accumulation Goal (Step #6) and divide it by your Annual Contribution Factor, which you get from the following chart, using the same number of years and investment return you used in Step #5.

ANNUAL CONTRIBUTION FACTORS

Number of years until you plan to retire	Compound annual investment return			
	4%	6%	8%	10%
5 years	5.416	5.637	5.867	6.105
10 years	12.006	13.181	14.487	15.937
15 years	20.023	23.276	27.152	31.772
20 years	29.778	36.785	45.762	57.274
25 years	41.645	54.864	73.105	98.346
30 years	56.084	79.057	113.282	164.491
35 years	73.651	111.432	172.314	271.018

Amount you need to save each year:

$________	÷	________	=	$________
Net RRSP Accumulation Goal (from Step 6)		Annual Contribution Factor		Yearly Savings Goal

This is the amount you need to save each year to reach your Net RRSP Accumulation Goal. If this amount is more than your Maximum Annual RRSP Contribution Limit, you should consider starting a non-registered investment plan to help you save the extra amount required to meet your goal.

Summary

You now have several important pieces of financial information. You've determined how much you need to contribute on an annual basis in order to reach your RRSP Accumulation Goal. Reaching this goal will provide you with the annual income you want from your RRSP savings during your retirement years.

Buying Your Own Software

You may come across various commercial software programs designed to help you manage your money and perhaps plan for retirement. Be warned that, like many of the financial planning books sold in Canada, most of the software packages you see on the shelves of your computer store are American. By and large, they're useless for Canadians. We have a different system of public pension programs, a different tax system, and even a different banking system. If you're not sure about a particular piece of software, check out who produces it and where the company is based. Don't waste your money on American software programs for retirement planning!

For Internet Junkies

If you're the type of person who is interested in the wonders of the Internet, you should know that most Canadian banks and some other financial institutions now have web sites on the Internet. If you're an Internet enthusiast, it's worth doing a bit of surfing to see what you can find. Scotiabank has one of the best bank home pages on the Internet (http://www.scotiabank.ca). There you'll find the Scotia RRSP Reality Check™—an interactive, personalized seven-page retirement savings report that's confidential—and free, too. This is a more sophisticated and personalized retirement planning exercise than the basic pencil-and-calculator one. You feed in some key details about yourself, such as your age, the age at which you plan to retire, the annual income you think you'll need in retirement, whether or not you belong to a workplace pension plan, and the amount you've already saved in your RRSP.

The information is then processed and you get a personalized report that tells you how much you'll need to save each year in your RRSP to meet your retirement savings goal, based on various assumptions about inflation, the rate of return you'll get on your RRSP investment, and so on. The program takes into account the maximum annual contribution limits for RRSPs and will tell you if you'll be able to meet your goal through RRSP savings, or if you'll have to look at other options. If it looks like you'll have a savings shortfall when you're ready to retire, there are several pages of suggestions about what you can do—for instance, increasing your investment return, saving outside your RRSP, or perhaps even reassessing your financial goals.

There is also a questionnaire to fill out if you want to know what kind of investor you are—whether you're a risk taker, a conservative investor, or somewhere in between. And there's a spreadsheet you can download to help you plan an investment program for yourself, based on your personalized profile and savings objectives.

Financial Advisers

If all this sounds too much like hard work and you'd like someone else to do it for you, you can get personalized advice from some financial institutions—often without charge. Royal Trust, for example, will do a basic run-through for you, once you answer some basic questions. The information is fed into the computer, which generates a savings target and tells you how much you'll need to save each year to reach it. Check at the local branch of your bank, trust company, or credit union to see if it has such a service. Some financial institutions will do a more detailed analysis for you for a small fee.

A qualified financial planner can do the same thing for you, but may charge you a fee. Some financial planners sell mutual funds and other financial products. Because they get commissions from sales, these planners don't charge a fee for financial advice. It goes without saying that they hope you'll buy the financial products they sell, so you need to be aware of that. A fee-for-service financial planner may charge more for retirement planning advice, but there's no chance of being pressured into investing.

The best way to find a good financial planner in your community is through personal recommendation. Ask your friends or colleagues if they can recommend someone, based on their own satisfactory experience. Failing that, you may want to check with one of the associations of financial planners, such as the Canadian Association of Financial Planners, the Canadian Institute of Financial Planning, or the Life Underwriters Association of Canada. These bodies recently formed an umbrella body called the Financial Planners Standards Council, which sponsors education courses leading to the Certified Financial Planner (CFP) designation. A qualified financial planner will have a CFP or comparable designation. These bodies, which should be listed in your phone book, should be able to give you a list of qualified planners in your own community, indicating which of them are strictly fee-for-service and which earn commissions from selling financial products.

Is it worth paying a financial planner to advise you on retirement planning? If you have a complex situation, a large estate that you want to leave to your children, business interests, or potential pension income from a variety of sources, the answer is probably yes. Financial planners charge by the hour and may also have a minimum charge. Depending on how complex your situation is and how much time is involved, expect to pay anywhere from $150 to several hundred dollars or more for one or two sessions. But if your situation is very complicated, it will be money well spent.

Understand Your Financial Situation

For financial planning, you can go it alone or get professional help. But even if you decide to get professional assistance with planning your future financial security, it's important that you yourself have a good understanding of how your retirement income will be generated. As a woman, it's particularly important to know what may happen to your plans for your pension if your family situation changes through separation, divorce, or death. The next few chapters will explain where the money may come from and how to cope if the unexpected happens.

CHAPTER 4

GOVERNMENT PROGRAMS

Nobody wants to be dependent on the government when they retire. But for women who are now retired, there wasn't much choice. Most of these women didn't have the opportunity to save for retirement or to accumulate pension benefits during their working years because they were working without pay in their homes. Many husbands didn't have a company pension, and even when there was one, it probably didn't allow for a benefit to be paid to the widow when her husband died. Some husbands, who had the option of providing a pension for a widow, decided against it so they could get a higher retirement pension during their lifetime. You can see it in the numbers. Women who are now aged 65 or older get 62 percent of their income from government programs and only 19 percent from their investments. And the percentage of income coming from investments is dropping as interest rates continue to slide. The average income of seniors who are women is only $14,845.

Of course, the world is changing. Most women now spend most of their adult years working for pay outside the home. Many now belong to company pension plans or contribute to RRSPs. But generally low earnings and interruptions in paid employment to have babies or take care of children and other dependent family members mean that government programs will probably still be an important part of retirement income for women coming up to retirement in the future. The big question is, just how much will you be able to count on government programs in the future? There's no doubt that these programs will come under the axe as governments slash spending to cope with deficits and fiscal restraint programs. What we don't know yet is how far and how deep governments will cut.

Government benefits are generally considered the first two tiers of Canada's three-tier retirement income system. In the first tier are programs like Old Age Security and the Guaranteed Income Supplement, which are funded from the general tax revenues of the government and intended to provide a basic guaranteed income for all seniors. The main objective of this part of the system is to prevent poverty. In the second tier is the Canada Pension Plan or, for residents of Quebec, the Quebec Pension Plan. These plans are paid for entirely by employer and employee contributions and provide a pension based on individual earnings and contributions. This part of the system is intended to replace a percentage of pre-retirement earnings so that people can maintain their standard of living after they retire. The third tier consists of tax-assisted private savings through workplace pension plans or RRSPs.

As discussed earlier, the usual rule of thumb is that your income in retirement needs to be about 70 percent of your pre-retirement income if you are to maintain the same standard of living as you had before retirement. Part of that 70 percent comes from the CPP, part from your employer pension plan (if you're lucky enough to have one), and part from your private savings through RRSPs and other investments. Part of that may also come from Old Age Security, but under a new system of benefits, which will come into effect in 2001, you can't count on that part any longer, as discussed on the next page.

The Anti-Poverty Programs

There are three programs in the first tier of the retirement income system: Old Age Security (OAS), the Guaranteed Income Supplement (GIS), and the Spouse's Allowance (SPA). These are all federal government programs, funded by the tax revenues of the federal government. All these programs are based on income—although it wasn't always so. While the GIS and SPA are income-tested, OAS is subject to a "clawback" for higher-income earners. Those whose income is above a certain threshold may receive a reduced OAS benefit or no benefit at all. More changes in this part of the system are coming. The government has already announced that OAS and GIS will be rolled into one income-tested benefit for seniors, starting in the year 2001. The SPA is to be retained as a separate program—at least for the time being. If you're already at or near retirement, you may continue to get your benefits under the existing system. If you're younger, you may be faced with a totally redesigned benefit by the time you're 65. Here's a look at what you can expect from these programs—both under the current system and under the proposed new Seniors Benefit scheduled for 2001.

Old Age Security

Old Age Security (OAS) has been around since the 1950s and has been a key benefit for women because it is not limited to those individuals who have participated in the paid work force. Even women who have never worked outside the home can get an OAS benefit in their own name when they reach the age of 65. In fact, many married women who have been full-time homemakers for most of their adult lives have seen their OAS benefit as at least a token recognition of the contribution their unpaid work has made. To be eligible for a benefit, the only stipulation used to be that you had to have lived in Canada for at least 10 years.

The OAS has been important to people who have been in the paid work force, too, because it has been one of the sources of retirement income that could be used to replace earnings when you retired. In the past, if your objective was to have an income in retirement that was about 70 percent of what you were making before the age of 65, knowing you could count on OAS to fill part of that quota meant you had to find less from other sources such as private savings or company pension plans. And since most women who were in the work force didn't have company pension plans or RRSPs, OAS has been particularly important for them.

When OAS was first introduced in the 1950s, benefits were roughly equivalent to 20 percent of the average wage, so someone whose earnings in the paid work force were about average could expect to get about 20 percent of those earnings replaced in retirement by OAS benefits. The OAS is indexed for inflation, but wages have increased faster than inflation—at least in the longer term. So while OAS has kept pace with inflation, it hasn't kept pace with wages. As a result, in mid-1996, the OAS benefit was equivalent to only about 13 percent of the average wage of about $35,400.

Because OAS is a flat-rate benefit (which was, until recently, unrelated to income), it represents a higher percentage of pre-retirement earnings for lower-income workers. A flat-rate monthly benefit of $400 represents almost 27 percent of earnings for someone who was making only $1,500 a month before retirement. But for someone who made $3,000 a month, the same flat-rate $400 monthly benefit replaces only about 13 percent of pre-retirement earnings. (In this chapter, the amounts of monthly benefits under various government programs have been rounded to the nearest dollar.) The structure of the benefit makes it particularly important for women, who are likely to earn less than the average wage, even when they work full-time for a full year. In 1994 (the year for which the latest data are available), the typical woman working in a full-time job earned about $28,400 a year. For someone earning that salary in 1996, OAS represented almost 18 percent of her pre-retirement earnings.

Until recently, the flat-rate OAS benefit was paid monthly to everyone at age 65—as long as they applied for it and met the residency requirement. The maximum monthly benefit in mid-1996 was $396. Although the amount of the OAS benefit is adjusted every three months with the increase in inflation, as measured by the Consumer Price Index (CPI), adjustments recently have been relatively small because there has been almost no inflation. Because OAS was available to everyone who met the age and Canadian residency requirements, regardless of income, OAS was described as a "universal" benefit.

But the rules began to change in 1977. Although the 10-year residence requirement is still in place, to receive the full monthly benefit at 65, you now must have lived in Canada for at least 40 years after the age of 18. That means if you're an immigrant, you may not qualify for the full OAS benefit. You'll get 1/40 of the full benefit for each year of residence after age 18 once you have satisfied the 10-year minimum residency requirement. That is, if you came to Canada when you were 40, you'd get only 62.5 percent of the full benefit if you apply at 65. Once a partial pension has been approved, it may not be increased as a result of added years of residence in Canada. Special provisions were made to cover immigrants in Canada who were 25 or older on July 1, 1977, when the new rules were introduced.

Canada does have social security agreements with 29 countries, including France, Germany, Italy, and Jamaica—but not the United Kingdom. Among other things, these agreements are intended to coordinate benefits between the two countries involved. If you come from one of the countries that has signed an agreement with Canada, you may be able to make up missing entitlements to Canadian benefits with benefits from your country of origin, or a country where you have lived or worked at some time during your life. You can get more information about this by calling your local income security office, listed in the blue pages of your phone book under Human Resources Development Canada.

More changes to Canada's Old Age Security program were put in place in 1989 when the federal government brought in a "clawback" to take benefits back from people whose income exceeded a certain threshold. Old Age Security has always been taxable, so anyone receiving it must include it in income and pay tax on it when filing a tax return. But until the clawback came in, the amount of the benefit paid did not depend on a person's income. Since 1989, however, seniors whose net incomes were $50,000 or more in that year have been required to pay back some or all of their OAS benefits. In other words, OAS is no longer a "universal" benefit.

Effectively, higher-income seniors can no longer count OAS benefits as part of their retirement income. But, because the threshold for the clawback has not been fully indexed for inflation, more and more pensioners have had to pay back OAS benefits as years go by and the level of the threshold falls further and further below what $50,000 was worth in 1989. For example, in 1996, anyone whose net income was $53,215 or more had to begin paying back some OAS benefits. But that $53,215 threshold was worth only about $45,000 in 1989 dollars. Even with relatively low rates of inflation, middle-income seniors will be affected by the clawback in a relatively short period of time.

More changes to OAS were announced in the 1995 federal budget. (Like all budget proposals, these changes have to be incorporated into legislation which must be passed by Parliament and receive royal assent before it becomes effective.) Instead of taking back OAS benefits from higher-income seniors when they filed their tax returns, the government said it would deduct any repayment due from monthly payments, starting in July 1996. And the government announced it would move toward a system of income-testing OAS, based on family income instead of individual income. "Family income," in this case, really means the income of both spouses. For example, if you're a widow living with adult children, your right to benefits will depend on your income alone. The incomes of the family members living with you will not be taken into account. But if you're married and living with your spouse, both your income and that of your spouse will be taken into account to determine if you're eligible for benefits. The family-income test will be introduced in 2001 when the new Seniors Benefit (described below) comes into effect.

For women, a family-income test for OAS is a major step backwards because it denies them economic autonomy. It also assumes that women have equal access to family income, which is not always the case—especially in families where there is wife abuse. A married woman's right to OAS, in most cases, will now depend on her husband's income, whether or not she works outside the home before retirement. That's because the average income of husbands usually far exceeds that of wives—even in retirement. So when you add a husband's income to a wife's, generally the husband's income will determine if either spouse gets OAS. The family-income test means that a woman who has spent most of her life as a full-time homemaker will no longer be able to count on an OAS benefit in her own name at 65. But it also means that women who spend most of their lives in the paid work force will not be able to count on an OAS benefit to meet part of their needs for replacement income in retirement.

In effect, the idea of OAS as a partial replacement for pre-retirement income has now been abandoned. It will be viewed strictly as an anti-poverty program and available only to those with modest incomes. The transition to a welfare program was completed with the 1996 federal budget, when the government announced that

OAS and GIS would be replaced with one income-tested Seniors Benefit—described below—starting in 2001, with the income test based on family income. Anyone who was aged 60 or older by December 31, 1995, would have the option of remaining under the old system of OAS and GIS.

Claiming Your OAS Benefit

Your OAS pension is not automatically sent to you when you reach the age of 65; you must apply for it. Your local Income Security Programs office, listed in the government section of the phone book under Human Resources Development Canada, can give you details. Generally speaking, to apply for OAS, you must be a Canadian citizen or a legal resident of Canada when the application is approved. You can also apply from outside the country, but if you apply from abroad, you must have been a Canadian citizen or legal resident of Canada immediately prior to your departure from Canada.

If you plan to go and live in another country when you retire, you may still be able to get your OAS pension. But, you will have to meet certain conditions. If you have lived in Canada for 20 years or more after the age of 18, your OAS benefit can be paid to you for the rest of your life, regardless of where you live. But if you have been in Canada for less than 20 years after age 18, you'll be able to get OAS outside Canada for the month in which you leave the country and the following six months only.

The pension is payable the month following the month in which all eligibility requirements are met. That may be the month after you turn 65 or the month after you meet the residency requirements. If you want to start the pension when you turn 65, you may want to apply some months in advance. But the Income Security Programs Branch says you should not submit an application earlier than 12 months in advance. If you're late in making your application, up to 12 months of retroactive payments can be made.

The Guaranteed Income Supplement

If you have very little income in retirement, you may qualify for the Guaranteed Income Supplement (GIS). This is a federal government program for people aged 65 or older whose incomes, not including OAS, are below a certain level. You can get GIS benefits only if you qualify for OAS. And the benefits are based on income only. That means you could have assets that do not produce any income, such as a home, and still qualify for GIS.

The GIS program pays different rates to single pensioners and married couples. The amount paid to a two-pensioner couple is less than the amount that two separate individuals would receive. The rationale for the difference is that two people together can save money by sharing expenses. But this rule only applies to two people who are married to each other or living common law. A same-sex couple or two relatives living together would be able to apply for GIS benefits as two separate individuals and would get more money than a married couple. Two individuals living together, based on rates in effect in mid-1996, could get a combined total of about $940 a month, compared with about $610 a month if the two people were a married couple.

The amount of the GIS benefit you get depends on your income and your marital status—the higher your income, the less you get. For a single pensioner, the formula is that for each $2 of income you have, not counting OAS, GIS is reduced by $1. Here's how it works. Suppose in June 1996 you were a single pensioner getting OAS, but you had no other income. You'd qualify for the maximum GIS benefit, which at that time was $470 a month, giving you a total income, including OAS and GIS of $865 a month. But what if you were getting OAS and a small pension of $200, a month? Your GIS benefits would then have been reduced to $370 a month ($470 minus half of $200), giving you a total income of $965 a month. As a single person at that time, you wouldn't have been eligible for GIS at all once your income—excluding OAS—reached $942 a month.

For married couples, GIS benefits are based on family income, although benefits are paid separately to each person. In mid-1996, if you and your spouse were both aged 65 or older and receiving OAS, you would have been entitled to some GIS as long as your joint income, excluding OAS, did not exceed $1,228 a month. For couples that qualified, the maximum monthly GIS benefit in June 1996 was $306 for each spouse ($612 for the couple).

Like OAS, GIS benefits are also fully indexed for inflation and are adjusted every three months in line with increases in the Consumer Price Index. But unlike OAS, GIS benefits are not taxable.

When it was first introduced, the GIS was intended to supplement OAS until the Canada/Quebec Pension Plan (described below) was completely in place. The CPP/QPP began in 1966, and policy makers expected that once those plans were fully phased in and employers had established private pension plans for their employees, few people would need to fall back on the GIS. But reality fell far short of those optimistic expectations. In fact, the GIS has become an important part of the social security system. Even pensioners entitled to maximum CPP/QPP retirement benefits still qualify for some GIS. For instance, the maximum CPP/QPP retirement benefit in 1996 was $727 a month, so a single person whose only retirement income was maximum OAS and maximum CPP/QPP would also have been entitled to GIS benefits of about $107 a month.

Because so many retired workers are not covered by private pension plans and don't have savings in RRSPs, many people are eligible for some GIS at the time of retirement. Others who are receiving very low benefits from private pensions and without inflation protection may qualify for GIS later in retirement, after inflation has eaten away at the value of their private pension plan benefits.

Applying for a GIS Benefit

You'll need to apply for GIS every year because it's based on your income. Application forms are mailed on request to everyone who is approved for OAS. If you qualify and start receiving GIS, you'll be sent a renewal application form in January each year. If you're over 65 and you don't currently receive GIS, but your circumstances have changed and you think you may be eligible, you may contact the Income Security Programs office for an application form. Up to 12 months of retroactive payments can be made if you're late in applying for GIS.

Usually, your previous year's income will determine your eligibility for GIS in the current year. If you're married or living in a common-law union, the income of both you and your spouse will have to be declared on the application form. Income that must be reported on the form includes CPP or QPP pensions, superannuation or private pension income, and other types of income, but excludes OAS. You can get a complete list of the types of income that must be reported from the Income Security Programs office. If you qualify for GIS, your payment will be included with your monthly OAS pension payment. Where both spouses qualify on the basis of family income, they each get payments in their own names. But if you don't send your renewal application form in by March 31, your monthly payment will revert to the basic OAS benefit for April, so it's important to fill out the form when you get it and send it back promptly.

If you or your spouse retired during the year or had a drop in private pension income, you can ask to have your eligibility for GIS based on your income, ignoring those previous earnings or higher pension income. This may create eligibility for GIS or may increase the amount of a GIS benefit already being paid. Again, the proper forms and advice for those individuals in this situation are available from the Income Security Programs office.

If you're getting GIS and you decide to leave the country, the benefit will be paid outside Canada for the month you leave and the following six months only. But payments may begin again if you return to Canada to live and you still meet the eligibility requirements.

The New Seniors Benefit

If you're still under 60, you may never get OAS or GIS benefits. That's because the federal government is about to introduce a new system of benefits for seniors. Starting in the year 2001, OAS and GIS, together with a couple of tax credits aimed at seniors and claimed on your income tax return, will be rolled into one income-tested Seniors Benefit. The tax credits are the age credit, which goes to taxpayers who are 65 or older and whose income is below a certain threshold; and the pension income credit, which is based on the first $1,000 of pension income from private retirement savings such as RRSPs, RRIFs, or workplace pension plans, but not including pension income from government programs such as OAS or CPP.

The changes were announced in the March 1996 federal budget, but the details have not yet all been made public. Whether you'll qualify for the new Seniors Benefit will depend on the joint income of you and your spouse—if you have one—although you'll still get your own payment in your name. The government says that couples who qualify for the new Seniors Benefit will each get separate and equal payments in their own names.

The amount of the new benefit will be roughly equivalent to the amount of the current OAS and GIS combined. Those who now get GIS or SPA will get an extra $10 a month above what they get under the current system. The new benefit will not be taxable, which is a change from the current system under which OAS is taxable, but GIS is not. The new benefit, like the existing OAS and GIS, will be fully indexed for inflation. The government estimates that anyone whose income is $45,000 a year or more—whether that's the joint income of two spouses or the income of a single individual—will get less money under the new system. Everyone who was aged 60 or over on December 31, 1995, and their spouses, no matter what age, will be guaranteed no less than current pension payments. In effect, they will be able to choose whether to remain under the current OAS/GIS system or move to the new Seniors Benefit.

If you're in your sixties, choosing whether to stay under the old system or move to the new one will not be easy. You can choose to receive OAS for the rest of your life and pay tax on it and you would also receive the non-taxable GIS if you qualify. The alternative is to opt for the new Seniors Benefit, which is not taxable. In either option, you would lose the age credit and the pension income credit. Although your income level may mean you'll get a lower benefit under the new system than you would under the old OAS/GIS, the fact that the new Seniors Benefit is not taxable may make up some or all of the loss. For instance, the National Council of Welfare estimates that if you're a single individual with an income of $25,000, you'd be entitled to a Seniors Benefit of $5,160 in the year 2001—exactly the same as you would have received under the existing OAS/GIS system. But because the new Seniors Benefit will not be taxed, the tax savings would translate into a net gain of $1,666 if you opt to move to the new system. If your income is $30,000, you'd lose $816 in benefits, but save $2,120 in taxes, for a net gain of $1,304 if you opt to move to the new system.

If you're part of a two-income couple, with a joint income of $25,000, your benefit will be the same under either system. But you'd save $3,170 in taxes by switching to the new system. You should note that, even if you opt to remain under the old system, your OAS benefit will be income-tested before it is paid, although the income test will still be based on individual income.

COMPARING THE NEW SENIORS BENEFIT TO THE TRANSITIONAL OPTION TWO-INCOME COUPLE, 2001

	Benefits Received			Income Taxes Paid			Overall
Outside Income	Taxable OAS plus GIS	Non-Taxable Seniors Benefit	Gain (Loss) in Benefits	Taxes under Transitional Option	Taxes under New System	Tax Savings	Gain (Loss)
None	$18,320	$18,440	$120	$0	$0	$0	$120
$5,000	15,820	15,940	120	647	0	647	767
$10,000	13,320	13,440	120	1,990	0	1,990	2,110
$15,000	10,820	10,940	120	3,333	683	2,649	2,769
$20,000	10,320	10,320	0	4,676	1,692	2,984	2,984
$25,000	10,320	10,320	0	6,019	2,849	3,170	3,170
$30,000	10,320	9,504	(816)	7,362	4,396	2,966	2,150
$35,000	10,320	8,504	(1,816)	8,705	5,933	2,772	956
$40,000	10,320	7,504	(2,816)	10,048	7,276	2,772	(44)
$45,000	10,320	6,504	(3,816)	11,756	8,619	3,137	(679)
$50,000	10,320	5,504	(4,816)	13,525	10,020	3,506	(1,310)
$60,000	10,320	3,504	(6,816)	17,065	13,559	3,506	(3,310)
$70,000	10,320	1,504	(8,816)	21,111	17,098	4,013	(4,803)
$80,000	10,320	0	(10,320)	25,219	20,979	4,329	(6,081)
$90,000	9,428	0	(9,428)	28,961	25,087	3,873	(5,555)
$100,000	8,528	0	(8,528)	32,915	29,235	3,680	(4,848)

Source: *A Guide to the Proposed Seniors Benefit.* A Report by the National Council of Welfare, Summer 1996.

The table on page 67, reproduced with permission from the National Council of Welfare's report, shows the choices that will face a two-income couple where at least one spouse was over age 60 on December 31, 1995.

In the table, the first column, "Outside Income," indicates any income either or both spouses may have from pensions, investments, employment, or other sources. The section of the table headed "Benefits Received" compares the benefits that the couple would receive if they opted to stay under the current system (receiving OAS and GIS) with the benefits they would receive if they opted for the new, non-taxable Seniors Benefit. Positive figures in the far right-hand column mean seniors would be better off with the new Seniors Benefit. Minus figures (in parentheses) mean they would be better off staying with Old Age Security. Even if they opted to remain under the current system, the couple would lose any tax credits for pension income or age to which they might have been entitled, because these credits will be abolished in 2001. The couple would also face an income test for their benefits, based on family income. By choosing to remain under the old system, the couple would receive OAS benefits, even if their joint income is $100,000. However, because these benefits are taxable, the couple will pay considerably more in taxes if they choose to remain under the existing system.

You can get the National Council of Welfare's free publication *A Guide to the Proposed Seniors Benefit* by writing to the organization at 2nd Floor, 1010 Somerset Street West, Ottawa, Ontario, K1A 0J9; calling (613) 957-2961; or faxing (613) 957-0680.

These decisions may be important to you if you're close to retirement and you don't expect to have much income from other sources such as workplace pensions and investments. But if you're a long way from retiring, the best way to take account of these changes in planning for your future financial security is to assume you won't get anything at all from this first tier of the retirement income system.

That means you'll have to save more for yourself. The objective of the new Seniors Benefit will be simply to act as a minimal safety net for those who have been unable to provide for themselves. And, of course, the objective of careful retirement planning is to make sure you have an adequate income in retirement so that you don't have to count on what will now be a basic social assistance program.

Provincial Supplements

Seniors who are really poor may also be able to get a provincial supplement to the federal programs. But not all provinces provide these benefits. Prince Edward Island, New Brunswick, Newfoundland, and Quebec do not have top-up programs for seniors. But the other six provinces, as well as the two territories do provide income supplements, generally for those who are getting the federal GIS. The amounts of these benefits vary from one province to another. And in most cases, the amount paid to married couples is more than double the amount paid to two separate individuals. If you're getting a GIS, you probably also qualify for a provincial supplement, if your province or territory has them. Check with your local income security office to find out.

The Spouse's Allowance Program

If you're in your sixties but not yet eligible for OAS (or the new Seniors Benefit) and you have very little income, you may be able to get a benefit through another federal program known as the Spouse's Allowance. It's a bit of a misnomer now because you don't have to be a spouse to get it. But you won't qualify if you've never been married or if you're divorced—no matter how low your income is. Nor will you qualify if you're aged 60 to 64 but married to someone who is not yet 65. If that seems unfair—it is. The Spouse's Allowance (SPA) program discriminates on the basis of marital status, and in a legal action that's slowly wending its way through the courts, the program is being challenged by several single and divorced women who believe it is contrary to the equality clauses of the Charter of Rights and Freedoms.

This is a program that was originally introduced to help spouses —mainly wives—of low-income pensioners. Women usually marry men who are older than they are, and in 1975, the federal government decided to do something to help women who were not yet 65 and who were married to low-income husbands already getting OAS and GIS. Although these couples had low incomes, the wives didn't yet qualify for OAS or GIS because they were too young. So the government introduced a benefit, roughly equivalent to OAS/GIS for the younger spouse, and called it the Spouse's Allowance.

That was fine as far as it went, but then problems started. If the older spouse died before the younger spouse had reached age 65, the Spouse's Allowance benefits were cut off, leaving the younger spouse with no alternative but social assistance. As an interim measure, the government decided to continue the benefits to the younger spouse for six months after the pensioner spouse's death. But that was just as bad, because six months after the husband died, the widow could still be cut off the program and not yet be eligible for OAS/GIS because she was under 65. To remedy that situation, in 1979, the federal government decided to continue benefits to the younger spouse after the pensioner spouse's death until the younger spouse reached the age of 65, at which point regular OAS/GIS would be payable.

Then in a fit of remorse about the penurious state of widows in his riding, then Minister of Health Jake Epp decided in 1985 to extend the Spouse's Allowance benefit to all widowed persons—male or female—aged 60 to 64 whose incomes are low enough to qualify for benefits, which means the widowed person no longer has to have been married to a low-income pensioner to qualify. A widowed person whose spouse had died before reaching the age of 65, or whose income while she or he was alive was too high to qualify for GIS, can still qualify for Spouse's Allowance. The only requirement is that the widow has income below a certain level. (The benefit is income-tested from the first dollar of other income and disappears completely at the threshold level of $15,456 annual income in mid-1996.) The deceased spouse might have died 30 years ago, but the widowed person who has not since remarried can qualify for Spouse's Allowance benefits once she or he reaches age 60. In other words, the program has become an income support program for individuals aged 60 to 64, but it's available only to those currently married to a low-income pensioner, or those who are widows and widowers and have not remarried (regardless of how long ago their spouses died).

Needy persons in the group aged 60 to 64 who are single, divorced, or married to someone under the age of 65 are not entitled to Spouse's Allowance, even though their incomes may be lower than those of a widowed person receiving benefits. For example, a woman aged 60 to 64 whose husband died 25 years ago and whose current income is $12,000 would qualify for a partial Spouse's Allowance benefit, as long as she has not remarried. A woman who was divorced 25 years ago and whose current income is only $10,000 would not qualify for the program.

Residence requirements for SPA are similar to those for OAS. The maximum monthly benefit is based on a combination of current OAS and GIS amounts and is indexed on a quarterly basis for inflation. There are two different rates for SPA benefits. For individuals aged 60 to 64 who are married to low-income pensioners, the amount of the SPA benefit is the same as the combination of OAS and GIS being received by the older spouse. In mid-1996, the maximum SPA benefit was $701.73 a month—the same as the maximum OAS/GIS available to each spouse in a low-income couple where both were aged 65 or older. The SPA benefit rates for widowed persons are higher than those for married people, but considerably lower than the amount of OAS and GIS combined that is available to single, divorced, or widowed pensioners aged 65 or older. The maximum SPA benefit for widowed persons in mid-1996 was $775 a month, compared with a maximum of $866 a month that was available to single, widowed, or divorced people who were aged 65 or older.

The 1996 federal budget announced that the SPA program will be continued, even after the new Seniors Benefit replaces the current OAS and GIS. In fact, people who qualify for SPA will get an extra $10 a month from 2001 on.

Claiming a Spouse's Allowance Benefit

Applying for a Spouse's Allowance works the same way as an application for GIS. The Income Security Programs Branch sends out application forms to OAS pensioners who are identified as having a spouse in the right age bracket. If you no longer have a spouse, but you're a widow aged 60 to 64, you can get an application form from the Income Security office.

Like GIS, SPA benefits are based on income from the previous year, and you will have to submit an application every year, as long as you're still in the age group for SPA benefits. Also, as with GIS, if you want to live somewhere else when you retire, SPA benefits will be paid outside Canada for the month of departure and for the following six months only. But benefits can be reinstated if you come back to Canada to live, as long as you still qualify.

The Income Replacement Programs

The second tier of the retirement income system is the government-sponsored Canada/Quebec Pension Plan, which provides benefits related to earnings. This part of the system has a clear objective: to replace a percentage of your pre-retirement earnings and help you maintain your standard of living in retirement.

Everyone in the paid work force who earns more than a minimum level of earnings, whether employed or self-employed, full-time or part-time, must contribute either to the Canada Pension Plan or the Quebec Pension Plan. Residents of Quebec contribute to the QPP; those in the rest of Canada contribute to the CPP. In most respects, the features of the two plans are the same. And the two plans are integrated so that if part of your working life is spent in Quebec and part elsewhere in Canada, your retirement pension and all other CPP benefits will be based on service and contributions to both plans, and the retirement benefit will be paid by the jurisdiction where you retire.

The government of Quebec operates the Quebec Pension Plan. But Quebec also has a say in the design of the CPP. For the rest of this chapter, we'll focus on the CPP, pointing out differences between it and the QPP where they're relevant. It's important to know that the CPP is not a federal government program, although it's governed by federal legislation. Changes to the plan can only be made with the approval of two-thirds of the provinces (including Quebec) having two-thirds of the population.

You've probably been hearing a lot about the Canada Pension Plan lately—claims that the plan is broke, that it won't be there when you retire, that it will have to be cut drastically because the government can no longer afford it, and that the level of contributions to the plan will have to go up so high to accommodate our aging population that people will no longer be willing to pay them. Every one of those statements is false—or at the very least, questionable and highly misleading. They're part of the extensive mythology that has grown up around the CPP—deliberately fostered in some quarters—that has undermined public confidence in the plan. The mythology will be dealt with in a moment. But, first a word about why the CPP is such a good deal for women.

Why the CPP Is Such a Good Deal for Women

The CPP is an ideal pension plan for women because it accommodates our lifetime work patterns and labour force participation—not to mention our greater life expectancy—much more effectively than the private pension system does.

It Doesn't Matter Where You Work

The CPP covers everyone, no matter in which sector of the economy people work. That's important because most women work in such sectors as community, business, and personal service, where few employers have pension plans. More and more women are working in what some economists have called "non-standard employment." These women get jobs through temporary help agencies and contract work, or they're working part-time even though they'd prefer a full-time job. Because they don't have a permanent relationship with an employer, women in these jobs generally don't have access to workplace pensions. And because many of these jobs are unstable and low-paying, those who do this kind of work find it difficult to save for their retirement through RRSPs. But the CPP covers everyone—even those in temporary jobs and who do contract work.

Overall, only 43 percent of women who have paying jobs belong to a registered pension plan through their work. Surprising as it may seem, most women who don't have workplace pensions don't contribute to RRSPs either. In 1993, for instance, only 27 percent of women above the age of 25 who didn't have a pension plan at work contributed to an RRSP. In other words, the private retirement income system doesn't cover a large percentage of women workers. That's why the CPP is such a vital part of women's future financial security.

It Covers You If You Work Part-Time or Are Self-Employed

The CPP covers all paid workers, regardless of whether they work part-time or full-time, or are self-employed. And part-time workers are covered, regardless of the number of hours they work. However, the first few thousand dollars of earnings—known as the

Year's Basic Exemption (YBE)—are exempt from CPP contributions. So, part-time workers who earned less than $3,500 in 1996 would have been excluded from making contributions to the CPP that year. And since most part-time workers are women, they're the ones who are most likely to be caught by this rule. Even so, the CPP still does a much better job of covering part-time workers than private pension plans do.

Until fairly recently, part-time workers generally were excluded from employer pension plans. In an attempt to include more women in private system coverage, pension laws, which govern the operation of these plans, were changed in the 1980s to require employers with pension plans for full-time workers to allow part-time workers to join. But most women who work part-time work for employers who don't have pension plans anyway. And given the option of joining a plan, many opt for cash in lieu of benefits if it's offered.

Self-employed individuals also must contribute to the CPP, generally when filing their income tax returns. This is also how temporary or contract workers make their contributions.

It Follows You When You Change Jobs

The CPP is completely portable—as people move from one job to another, it moves with them. No matter where you work or how many times you change jobs, you're covered. This feature is particularly important for women who have tended to be more mobile workers—sometimes withdrawing from the work force for periods of time to raise children, or changing jobs in search of better pay and prospects.

The same options don't really apply to the private pension system. If you change jobs, you may be able to move your accumulated pension benefits to a new employer or even transfer them out of the pension plan to a locked-in retirement account. But this is still not always possible and, in any case, these rules were implemented only recently and were not retroactive to benefits earned prior to the

1980s when the laws changed. If you belong to a company pension plan and you quit to go to work for another employer, you may have to leave part of your pension benefits behind in your former employer's plan. And while you may get some kind of pension based on those accumulated benefits when you reach retirement, the pension may not be worth very much by then.

You're Not Penalized If You Quit Work to Have Children

If you have to quit work to raise your family, the CPP makes allowances. The CPP retirement benefit is based on the individual's average annual earnings over the period from the age of 18 to the age of 65. The CPP accommodates the child-rearing responsibilities of women by allowing contributors to exclude from the calculation any periods during which they had a child under the age of seven. In this way, non-income or low-income years caused by child-rearing will not drag down the lifetime average earnings. This means that women are not penalized in terms of retirement income if they leave the paid work force to bear and raise children, or work part-time while their children are young.

Such a feature is almost unknown in the private retirement income system. Women who have no earned income, for example, are not allowed to contribute to an RRSP. And while some private pension plans allow workers who withdraw from the paid work force for a period of time to make up lost contributions to the workplace pension plan when they return, the cost of doing so has often proved prohibitive for women returning from maternity or child-care leave. In the federal public service plan, for instance, until very recently, women returning from child-care leave were required to pay triple contributions to the plan—their own current contributions, their own contributions for the period they were on leave, and their employer's contributions for the leave period—all at a time when these women faced additional expenses for child care. Many women couldn't afford to return to the public service when their leave ended because they couldn't afford to make these mandatory contributions.

You Get a Share in Your Spouse's Benefits on Marriage Breakdown

If you divorce or separate, you're entitled to share in the CPP credits your spouse built up during your marriage—even if you didn't work outside the home while you were married. This is one way full-time homemakers can acquire a CPP benefit in their own names, even though they have never contributed to the CPP themselves. But it's also a way of equalizing benefits between spouses where both have been in the work force but one has accumulated a much lower CPP pension. Given women's much lower earnings, it is generally women who benefit from this provision in the CPP. Division of pensions between spouses on divorce is still a thorny issue in most private pension plans. Many spouses at divorce give up their right to a share in a spouse's employer-sponsored pension in exchange for other assets. This may simplify the financial arrangements for divorcing spouses and avoid some of the hassle, but it may also result in a divorced wife having no pension, except for those from government programs, at retirement.

Changes made to the CPP a few years ago were supposed to make credit-splitting mandatory on divorce or legal annulment. But the CPP legislation passed by Parliament allows credit-splitting to be overridden by provincial family law. Saskatchewan and British Columbia subsequently decided to override the federal law and allow spouses to waive their right to division of CPP pension credits at marriage breakdown. Couples in Quebec can also decide not to have their QPP credits split on marriage breakdown.

The automatic credit-splitting came about because few women were taking advantage of the credit-splitting provision. Prior to the changes, you had to apply for division of CPP credits within three years of the breakdown of the marriage. Many women were apparently unaware of the provision. Many others gave up their right to a share in a husband's CPP credits in exchange for other assets. Women's groups and others urged the federal government to make credit-splitting on divorce mandatory and automatic. As a result, the rules were changed in 1987 to eliminate the need for a formal application for division of credits. In theory, at least, CPP credits are now divided as soon as the Income Security Programs Branch of Human Resources Development Canada is aware of the divorce and has all the relevant information. If you're in the process of divorcing, it's important to notify the authorities of your divorce so they can arrange for you to be credited with your share of your spouse's accumulated CPP. But don't forget that you will have to share your benefits with him, too. If you've both been contributing to the plan, the objective is to give you equal benefits based on the period you were together. The credits you receive as a result of credit-splitting become part of your record of earnings permanently, and are used to determine your eligibility for other CPP benefits, such as disability benefits and survivor benefits, as well as to determine the amounts of these benefits you may receive.

Common-law spouses are also eligible for division of pension credits on the breakdown of their relationship. But they have to apply for a division, and they can't do that until they have been living apart for one year. They then have three years from that point in which to apply for the division.

You May Also Share Your Spouse's Benefits at Retirement

Spouses in an ongoing relationship may also share their accumulated CPP retirement pension when both reach retirement age, regardless of whether one or both spouses have contributed to the plan. This is another feature that enables a spouse who has not worked outside the home to receive a CPP retirement benefit in her own name. It's a provision that was introduced mainly to respond to those who felt that women who had not worked outside the home should be entitled to their own benefits from the CPP in recognition of their contribution to the marriage. Such a feature is unheard of in private pension plans. (Until recently, it was not available for members of the QPP either.) Both spouses must be at least 60 years old and must have applied for any CPP retirement pension to which they may be entitled. That is, you can't arrange for benefit-splitting until both spouses have retired. If, for instance, your husband retires but you're still working, he won't be able to share his pension with you until you also retire.

Benefit-splitting at retirement—technically known as "assignment"—is still available only on a voluntary basis and the take-up rate has been low. That's surprising, since dividing CPP benefits between spouses at retirement is one of the few ways couples can split their income and reduce their taxes. It's a strategy that's often recommended by financial planners, but it only works if one spouse has much lower income than the other and if transferring benefits to the lower-income spouse would reduce the income tax liability of the higher-income spouse.

Some women's groups have advocated that division of CPP credits at retirement be mandatory, and this option seems to have been raised again during the current debate about changes to the CPP. While it might help some women, you could also argue that it undermines the economic autonomy of women (and men, too, for that matter) by forcing them to share income with a spouse. Benefit-splitting at retirement won't increase the total CPP benefits payable to a couple, but in most situations it will improve the CPP retirement benefit payable to a married women in her own name because she is likely to have had lower lifetime earnings than her husband or may even have had no earnings at all.

If you apply for this kind of sharing under the CPP, you and your spouse will each receive a portion of the other's CPP retirement pension, if there is any. The portion will be calculated using the length of time you lived together in relation to your total contributory period. For instance, if you lived together for 20 percent of your contributory period, each of you would keep 80 percent of your own retirement pensions, and the remaining 20 percent would be shared between you.

You should also know that sharing CPP benefits at retirement is only a temporary arrangement, that ends when one spouse dies, in the month a couple gets divorced, or a year after the couple separates. You can also cancel the arrangement if you submit a written request from both spouses; but either spouse may then submit a written request to have the assignment reinstated.

When either partner dies, the retirement and survivor benefits paid to the survivor will be based on the benefits each spouse was entitled to before the sharing took place. Often, that's advantageous to women, because they generally outlive their husbands and their pensions are likely to be lower. For example, if you're 65 or older when your husband dies, you'd be entitled to a surviving spouse benefit that's 60 percent of what he was getting as a retirement pension. As well, under a pension assignment arrangement, if he dies, you'd get 60 percent of his benefit before assignment, not 60 percent of his share of the split pension.

You're Protected Against Inflation

The CPP is fully indexed for inflation—an important feature for women, who generally live longer than men. Few private pension plans are routinely indexed, although many plans do provide ad hoc inflation adjustments at the discretion of the plan sponsor. Retirement pensions from the CPP are adjusted each year by the full amount of the increase in the Consumer Price Index.

The Retirement Age Is Flexible

The CPP also provides a flexible retirement age: it can be anywhere between the ages of 60 and 70. This allows women and men who retire prior to the age of 65, as most do, to claim a somewhat reduced CPP benefit. If you retire before 65, your pension will be reduced by one-half of 1 percent for each month before your 65th birthday. If you retire at 60, for example, your CPP retirement pension would be only 70 percent of what you'd get if you retired at 65. And the benefit will not be increased when you turn 65. If you retire between the ages of 65 and 70, your pension will be increased at the same rate. If you start receiving your benefit at 68, say, your pension will be 18 percent higher than you would have received if you'd started getting the pension at 65.

In 1996, when the maximum CPP benefit for someone retiring at 65 was $727 a month, the maximum for a person retiring at the age of 60 was $509 a month, while the maximum for a person retiring at the age of 70 was $945 a month.

You Get a Pension If Your Spouse Dies

The CPP has surviving-spouse benefits so that when your husband or partner dies, you're entitled to a percentage of his CPP pension. While the laws governing private pension plans now also require such plans to provide surviving-spouse benefits, spouses may waive the right to these benefits, as long as they both agree in writing to do so. Of course, if you waive the right to survivor benefits when your husband retires, you may benefit from sharing a higher retirement income with him as long as he lives, but you'll be left with nothing when he's gone.

To be eligible for a CPP surviving-spouse benefit, your spouse must have contributed to the CPP in at least one-third of his "eligible years" (between the age of 18 and the age at which CPP retirement benefits begin) or for 10 years, whichever is lower. If you are 65 or older when your spouse dies, you'll get a pension that's 60 percent of his retirement pension or 60 percent of the retirement pension he would have received had he turned 65 on the date of death. If you are under 65 when he dies, you'll get a flat-rate amount, plus 37.5 percent of the retirement benefit he would have been entitled to had he turned 65 on the date of death.

Benefits paid by the QPP for surviving spouses under the age of 65 are considerably more generous. The QPP has a lower benefit for spouses under the age of 55 than for spouses over that age, but both are much higher than the corresponding CPP benefits.

Surviving-spouse benefits are not paid to surviving spouses under the age of 45 unless they are disabled or they have dependent children. And in both the CPP and QPP, when a surviving spouse reaches 65, her benefit is reduced to 60 percent of the deceased contributor's retirement pension.

If you're entitled to a CPP surviving-spouse benefit as well as to a CPP pension in your own name, the two benefits together cannot exceed the maximum retirement benefit payable at the age of 65. Even though a surviving-spouse benefit for widows aged 65 or older is only 60 percent of what the deceased spouse would have received, you may get a higher CPP pension as a surviving spouse than you would as a contributor to the plan in your own right. That's because men's earnings, on which almost all surviving-spouse benefits are based, are so much higher than the earnings of women. For instance, women who started claiming retirement pensions in their own right in July 1996 got an average benefit of $286 a month. Women who started receiving surviving-spouse benefits in the same month averaged $292 a month. Once you start receiving a surviving-spouse benefit, it will continue for the rest of your life, even if you remarry. (Surviving-spouse benefits are described in more detail in Chapter 7.)

You Get a Lump-sum Benefit When Your Spouse Dies

The CPP pays a lump-sum death benefit when a contributor dies. This part of the program was originally intended to help pay for funeral expenses, but it is one of the features of the CPP that may be eliminated in the current round of discussions on changes to the CPP.

More than 70 percent of CPP death benefit claims are made on the death of male contributors—which means most of those receiving these lump-sum benefits are probably widows. For both the CPP and the QPP, the amount of the death benefit is equal to the lesser of six times the monthly retirement pension or 10 percent of that year's maximum pensionable earnings (YMPE). In 1996, the maximum death benefit for both the CPP and the QPP was $3,540. But in July 1996, the average lump-sum benefit paid on the death of male contributors to the CPP was $2,803, while the average paid on the death of female contributors was $1,961.

Dependent Children May Get Benefits If Parents Die

If you have dependent children, they may get benefits from the CPP if you or your spouse die or become disabled. Sometimes referred to as "orphan" benefits, these are flat-rate benefits paid to the dependent children of a deceased contributor. Dependent children of a contributor who becomes disabled may be entitled to a "disabled contributor's child's benefit." The same amount is paid, regardless of the age of the child. And, if both you and your husband were contributing to the CPP and both of you died at the same time and left dependent children, they would be entitled to two "orphan" benefits—one from you and one from their father. In the CPP, the amount of a dependent child's or orphan's benefit, which was $164 monthly in 1996, is fixed annually. In the QPP, the monthly benefit is $52. The reason for the lower benefit in the QPP is that Quebec has other benefits for children that are more generous than those paid in the rest of Canada. The QPP doesn't pay benefits to children above age 18.

Dependent children are defined as: children under the age of 18; children between the ages of 18 and 25 if they are in full-time attendance at school, college, university, or some other types of educational institutions; or children above the age of 18 who are disabled.

The CPP and Income Replacement

If there's one problem with the CPP, it's that benefit levels are low in relation to earnings. The amount of the retirement pension is equivalent to 25 percent of a worker's average annual lifetime earnings, up to a maximum equivalent to the average wage. With roughly 18 percent of pre-retirement earnings coming from OAS and 25 percent from the CPP, the average woman with a full-time job will still have to find another 27 percent of her pre-retirement earnings from somewhere else if she wants to maintain her standard of living in retirement. And that's a problem because most women don't have an employer pension plan or an RRSP to fill the gap.

When the CPP/QPP was established in 1966, the earnings replacement rate was deliberately set low because policy makers expected workplace pension plans would come to play an important income replacement role in the retirement income system. However, that hasn't happened. In 1993, private pensions, including workplace pensions and RRSPs, accounted for only 15 percent of the income of women who were seniors. In contrast, 62 percent of their income came from government transfer payments.

Women who retired in 1996 and started getting their CPP retirement pensions in July of that year received an average of only $286 a month, compared with an average of $505 a month being paid to men who retired at the same time. One reason for the lower amount was that more women than men retired before the age of 65 and therefore had to make do with a lower pension than they would have had if they'd waited until the age of 65. But the most important reason women got lower benefits from the CPP is that, overall, women had lower earnings while they were working. In 1995, about 28 percent of all employed women worked part-time. And even women with full-time jobs earn much less than men, on average.

That has led some people to conclude that the CPP is not such a good deal for women after all, because the pensions they get are so low. But it's important not to lose sight of the fact that the CPP is intended to be an income replacement plan. Because women have low earnings, an income replacement pension plan—especially one that pays only 25 percent of pre-retirement earnings—will give them low benefits. One way to address this problem would be to look at ways of improving women's earnings through measures such as pay equity.

The CPP and You

So the CPP is generally a good plan for women. Here are a few other basic features of the plan that you need to know about.

What You Have to Contribute

If you're an employee, your contribution to the CPP will be deducted automatically from your pay, and your contribution is matched by one from your employer. If you're self-employed, you pay both parts yourself—usually when you file your income tax return. The contribution rate is set by the government as a percentage of your "contributory earnings." Each year, there's a "Year's Basic Exemption" (YBE) that exempts you from making contributions on the first few thousand dollars of your earnings. And there's a "Year's Maximum Pensionable Earnings" (YMPE), which is the upper limit of earnings on which contributions have to be made. The YMPE is equivalent to the average wage. Both YBE and YMPE are adjusted annually to reflect wage and salary increases. For 1996, the YBE was $3,500 and the YMPE was $35,400. In other words, your CPP contributions are made only on the part of your earnings that are between $3,500 and $35,400, known as your contributory earnings. If you earned $20,000 in 1996, for example, your CPP contribution would be a percentage of $16,500 ($20,000 – $3,500).

Federal and provincial governments have set CPP contribution rates 25 years ahead to take account of the aging of the population. The rates are reviewed every five years and changed, if necessary, based on experience. For 1996, employers and employees each contributed 2.8 percent of contributory earnings, or a maximum of $893.20 each. If you were self-employed, you paid 5.6 percent of contributory earnings, or a maximum of $1,786.40.

How Retirement Benefits Are Calculated

The monthly retirement pension you'll get from the CPP will be equivalent to 25 percent of your average monthly pensionable earnings over your working life—defined as from the age of 18 to the age of 65, or from the age you were in 1966 to the age of 65 if you were already 18 or older in 1966 when the CPP began. But your actual pensionable earnings are adjusted upward to reflect the growth in the YMPE over the years. That's done so that your pension will not be based on outdated wage and salary levels. (It should be noted that the "pensionable earnings" on which your retirement pension will be based include all your earnings up to the YMPE. "Contributory earnings," on the other hand, exclude earnings below the YBE.) Once your CPP pension starts, it will be fully indexed to the cost of living, as measured by the Consumer Price Index.

Child Raising and Other Exclusions

If your CPP retirement pension is based on all the years between 18 and 65, what if you were at university until the age of 21, or you were out of work for long periods during that time? The CPP allows you to exclude up to 15 percent of the years from 18 to 65, or roughly seven years, from the calculation of average annual earnings on which your retirement pension will be based, to cover this kind of situation. You can choose years in which you had low earnings or no earnings at all. All this will be done for you automatically when you apply for your CPP retirement benefit.

But as well as this 15 percent exclusion that everybody gets, when you're calculating average earnings on which your pension will be based, you can also exclude periods when you had a child under the age of seven. Again, this will be done at the point when you apply for your pension. This provision is often referred to as the "child-rearing drop-out," which seems to have led to quite a bit of confusion. "Drop-out" simply refers to the fact that you drop these years out of the calculation of average earnings. It doesn't mean you have to have dropped out of the work force when you had your children. The idea is that you will not be penalized if you made low or zero earnings while your children were little. If you could only work part-time or part of the year when your children were young, your pension will not be reduced because of these family responsibilities.

In a two-parent family, only one spouse may take advantage of this option. In the past, this was usually the spouse who received the family allowance on behalf of the child. Now that family allowances have been abolished, you can prove your eligibility for the CPP child-rearing provision by demonstrating eligibility for the Child Tax Benefit (CTB). And you should know that even if your income was too high to get the CTB, you're still eligible to claim the child-rearing drop-out provision because you were potentially eligible to get the CTB if your income had been lower.

Are You Eligible for a CPP Pension?

Even if you've made only one monthly contribution to the CPP, you'll be able to get a retirement pension—but, of course, it won't be worth very much. Your salary for the month you contributed would be averaged over your entire working life and your pension would be worth 25 percent of that annual average. Obviously, the longer you have worked and made contributions to the plan, the better your pension is likely to be. As explained earlier, you can claim your CPP pension any time between the ages of 60 and 70. But if you claim it before you turn 65, you will have to demonstrate that you've "wholly or substantially" stopped working when you make the claim. Once you start getting the pension, though, there's nothing to stop you from going back to work, although you will not be able to make any more CPP contributions, so you'll be stuck with a lower pension than if you had continued to work until the age of 65. You're allowed to receive CPP retirement benefits while you're working part-time as long as you earn less than the CPP maximum retirement pension payable at age 65, which in 1996 was $727 a month.

You must apply for your CPP pension—the benefits are not paid automatically. And you'll be able to get the maximum benefit if you have earned at least as much as the YMPE each year since 1966, when the plan started, or since the age of 18 if you were under 18 when the CPP began. Even if your earnings were lower, you may still be able to qualify for the maximum pension by using the "drop-out" periods described above. Once you start receiving your CPP pension, it can be paid to you anywhere in the world. So even if you go to live in another country when you retire, you'll still be able to get your CPP pension.

Disability Benefits

The CPP also pays a monthly pension to those who have contributed to the plan and are disabled, in accordance with CPP rules. That is, your disability can be physical or mental, but it must be "severe and prolonged." "Severe" means your condition prevents you from working regularly at any job, and "prolonged" means your condition is long-term or may result in your death.

To be eligible for disability benefits, you must have contributed to the CPP for two of the past three years or five of the past 10 years when you become disabled. Even if you haven't contributed for enough years at the time you apply, you may still be able to qualify, for example, if: you are also entitled to the child-rearing drop-out; you acquired pension credits from your former spouse when your marriage broke up; or you worked in another country with which Canada has a social security agreement and you contributed to that country's plan. There may be other reasons, too. You can get more information about this by contacting your Income Security Programs office, listed in the phone book under Human Resources Development, Government of Canada.

The disability pension is made up of two parts: a flat-rate amount and an amount based on how much and for how long you paid into the CPP. The maximum CPP disability pension in 1996 was $870.92 a month, or about $10,450 a year, compared with the maximum retirement benefit of about $8,725 a year.

Will the CPP Still Be There for You?

This is all very well, you may be saying, but how do I know if the CPP will be there when I get to retirement? Everyone says the plan is running out of money and that there will be nothing left by the time the baby boom generation retires, in the early years of the next century. Many people seem to be worried about the future of the CPP. But a lot of the worry seems to be based on misinformation and myth. The CPP is not "running out of money" because it's a "pay-as-you-go" plan. It's not set up like a private workplace pension plan, where employees contribute to a fund, which is invested in the stock market and used to pay their pensions. CPP pensions are not paid from a pot of money that is rapidly dwindling away as more and more seniors start claiming benefits. A pay-as-you-go system, which is the way public pension programs in almost all industrialized countries work, means that the contributions coming in from people in the work force go to pay the benefits of those who are retired. To ensure there will be enough money to pay the benefits as retirees form an increasing percentage of Canada's population, the federal and provincial finance ministers who are responsible for running the CPP have already set contribution rates for the next 25 years, and they're scheduled to increase gradually over that time to accommodate the increasing demands on the plan as the baby boom generation moves into retirement. That's why it's meaningless to claim that "the CPP is running out of money." However, at the heart of the current debate about the CPP is how high those contribution rates will have to go and whether people 35 years from now will be prepared to pay the higher rates.

It's also meaningless to claim that the plan has "unfunded liabilities," like a private pension plan. Private pension plans set up by employers are required to have a fund set aside to pay the benefits so that employees can be sure they'll get a pension, even if the employer is no longer around when they retire. Those considerations don't apply to a public pension program, where the government is responsible for making sure those individuals who contribute to the program get a pension at retirement. Public plans are almost always set up on a pay-as-you-go basis because of the assumption that the government is always going to be around. Besides, many people argue that if we had to have a fund set aside to pay CPP pensions, we'd have billions of dollars under government control, which most people don't think is very desirable.

When the federal and provincial finance ministers set up the current 25-year rate schedule in 1985, they agreed to meet every five years to review the schedule and to extend it by a further five years. They also agreed to establish rates at a level that would bring in enough money to pay all the benefits as well as to generate a reserve fund equivalent to two years' worth of benefits. This fund is used as a contingency reserve in case contribution revenue is less than expected. If this happens, contribution rates can be adjusted again at the next five-year rate review. Provinces are allowed to borrow from this reserve fund in proportion to the contribution revenue generated in the province, at a rate of interest comparable to that paid on long-term Government of Canada bonds.

Given that the 25-year rate schedule provides for CPP contribution rates to increase gradually each year, the idea of having to increase contributions to maintain the plan is nothing new. However, during the regular five-year review in 1996 the government apparently decided that the rates projected for the year 2030 were too high. The government has suggested that, instead of increasing rates gradually over the next 40 or 50 years, it will increase them very sharply over the next six years. That would bring in more than enough money to pay the benefits. In fact, it would bring in enough to allow the establishment of a bigger reserve fund, which would contain about six years' worth of benefits. Instead of simply serving as a contingency reserve, this much bigger fund, which would probably amount to about $120 billion, would be invested in the capital market. The earnings on the fund, together with the contribution revenue, would be enough to pay all the benefits for the foreseeable future, without ever having to increase contribution rates again—at least that's the theory behind it.

The government says that to have such a fund and still have enough money coming in to pay all the benefits would require a combined contribution rate of 12.2 percent. But the business community doesn't want to see contribution rates any higher than 10 percent. That means cuts will probably have to be made in benefits to keep the contribution rate down and still have enough coming in to set up the investment fund. Of course, cutting back CPP benefits has nothing to do with restraining government spending, because no government funding is in the CPP. In fact, the legislation prohibits it. The benefits are financed entirely by contributions from employers and employees, together with interest earned on the reserve fund.

A number of changes have been proposed to cut the cost of benefits. Almost all of them would affect women more than men. They include the following:

- Cutting the basic CPP retirement pension by 10 percent, so that it replaces only 22.5 percent of earnings up to the maximum, instead of the current 25 percent.
- Raising the age of eligibility from 65 to 67, and the age at which you could claim early retirement pensions from 60 to 62.
- Reducing the number of years that could be "dropped out" to calculate average earnings, on which your pension will be based.
- Putting some restrictions on the child-rearing drop-out.
- Putting a cap on indexing, so that the retirement pension would be indexed only to increases in the Consumer Price Index minus one percentage point.
- Putting further restrictions on benefits for surviving spouses. The government apparently believes that since more women are now in the paid work force, they won't need surviving spouse benefits when their spouses die because they'll have good pensions in their own right!
- Getting rid of the lump-sum death benefit.
- Restructuring disability benefits to make them less costly.

Choosing just one of these options will not be enough to reduce the combined contribution rate to the desired level and still have an investment fund. So chances are that the finance ministers will select a package of these options. There has been no analysis of the impact these proposals will have on the incomes of future seniors, but you can be sure the changes will affect the kind of benefit you can expect from the CPP in the future.

Public opinion polls show strong support for the continuation of the CPP as Canada's public pension program. And the good news is that the federal and provincial governments clearly intend to continue the plan, even though they have been urged by the Reform Party and others to get rid of it and replace it with a system of compulsory RRSPs. It's safe to say that the CPP will be there when you retire, but it may provide even less in the way of benefits than it does now.

The direction of the proposed changes is clearly to shift much more of the responsibility—and the risk—of providing for retirement on to individuals. Canada's collective responsibility for and to its seniors is undoubtedly being weakened.

What does it all mean for your retirement planning? It means you will have to do much more on your own, and that won't be easy. Major changes to the CPP are unlikely to be retroactive. But for younger people, now more than ever, you will have to save as much as you possibly can, to make sure your financial future is secure.

CHAPTER 5

YOUR EMPLOYER

Everyone has to contribute to the Canada Pension Plan if they have a paying job. But some people may also belong to a private pension plan, provided in their workplace. Workplace pension plans may be sponsored by an employer or a group of employers, or sometimes by a trade union. It's important to find out if you're covered and, if you are, to know what kind of plan you have. When you have that information, you'll be in a better position to see how much more you'll need to save on your own to have enough money to live on in retirement.

Employees who accumulate benefits in a pension plan are considered members of that plan. More and more women now belong to workplace pension plans, although these private pension arrangements still only cover less than half of all employed women. If you work for any level of government, you are almost certainly covered. If you work for a large employer, you probably have a workplace pension plan. You're more likely to be covered if you work in certain sectors of the economy, such as manufacturing or telecommunications. And if you're a member of a union, you're also more likely to have a workplace pension plan.

Generally, where a pension plan is provided, membership in the plan is compulsory—it's a condition of your employment. But you may or may not have to contribute to the plan. Some workplace pension plans are financed entirely by the employer. They are known as "non-contributory" plans because employees don't have to contribute. Of course, the fact that you are provided with a pension plan is taken into account when your salary level is established. That's why many workers regard workplace pension plans as "deferred wages"—even if the employees don't have to pay into the plan, they have given up something in wages because the plan is there.

As will be explained in more detail later, even if you don't make any contributions to the pension plan yourself, belonging to a workplace pension plan will limit the amount you can contribute to an RRSP. If your workplace pension plan is a non-contributory one, you may not even be aware you have pension coverage—or perhaps you were told about it when you were hired and have forgotten the details. Just the same, it's important to find out what kind of pension plan you have. The benefits you'll get at retirement could play a key role in ensuring your financial security in your senior years.

There are many different kinds of pension plans. Finding out what kind you have and what sorts of benefits it provides may not be easy. In this chapter, the various types of workplace pensions and the kinds of benefits you can expect from them will be examined.

What Kind of Pension Plan Do You Have?

The terms and conditions of your membership in your pension plan are spelled out in the documents issued by the sponsor of the plan. If your employer has a pension plan, you probably got a booklet about it when you were hired. But employee pension plan booklets are notoriously difficult to read. Some are written in incomprehensible jargon, although some employers are making progress in developing information about their pension plans that is more reader-friendly. The best way to find out what kind of workplace pension plan you have is to ask your employer's human resources department or your union representative if you're a member of a union.

While there are all kinds of pension plans, only some of them guarantee you a benefit at retirement. Other retirement income arrangements may be described as a "pension plan," but are actually just RRSPs to which your employer contributes. What you need to know is that there are basically three main types of pension arrangements: "defined benefit" plans, "defined contribution" plans, and group RRSPs. These are described in detail later in this chapter. Strictly speaking, only the first two of these are really pension plans. Although group RRSPs are becoming increasingly popular with employers, this type of plan is simply a way for the employer to give you a hand in setting aside some money for your retirement in an RRSP, along with the other employees, and the amounts contributed have to be included in your regular RRSP contribution limit.

Workplace pension plans, whether they are defined benefit plans or defined contribution plans, have to be registered with Revenue Canada so that both you and your employer can claim a tax deduction for contributing to the plan. That's why they're sometimes called Registered Pension Plans (RPPs). The Revenue Canada rules also limit the maximum pension that a Registered Pension Plan may provide and the maximum contribution that may be deducted each year for tax purposes. That's because giving people a tax deduction means the government loses tax revenue, so Revenue Canada's rules are a way of controlling the cost of these measures in lost tax revenues.

When Can You Retire and Collect Your Workplace Pension?

Your workplace pension plan may set out a "normal retirement age," which is the age at which you would normally start drawing your pension. It's generally 65, but the law does not allow it to be any later than your 66th birthday. In fact, you can choose to retire at any age, as long as you are not more than 10 years younger than the normal retirement age. But, of course, if you decide to retire early, your pension will be lower than if you continued working until the normal retirement age. Early retirement would mean not only that you would have fewer years of service and less time to build up your entitlement to a pension, but also that you would have to live longer in retirement on the lower pension.

Some workplace pension plans allow you to postpone your retirement and to continue accumulating pension benefits. But if you decide to go on working after starting your pension, you will not be allowed to build up any additional pension benefits.

Pension Standards Laws

Like other workplace standards, the terms and conditions of Registered Pension Plans are established by provincial governments. The federal government regulates pension plans for workers who are under federal jurisdiction, such as those who work for banks, transportation companies, and telecommunications firms. Pension plans for workers in the public sector are generally governed by special acts of the provincial legislature or the federal Parliament. For instance, the pension plan for people who work for the federal government is governed by the federal Public Service Superannuation Act. Group RRSPs, because they are not really pension plans, do not fall under federal and provincial pension standards laws, although group RRSPs are subject to Revenue Canada's rules for tax purposes, as are all other RRSPs.

Pension standards laws, which may vary slightly from one province to another, make sure workplace pension plans meet certain minimum standards. These laws specify what kind of investments the pension plan may invest in, when your pension benefits are "vested," whether part-time workers have to be given the option to join the plan and how "part-time" work is defined, what rights you have when you terminate your employment, and so on. Your own particular pension plan may have slightly different provisions, but it must meet the minimum standards set by the regulatory authority where the plan is located.

To find out what laws apply to your pension plan, you may contact your province's pension commission, which should be listed in the phone book under your provincial government. However, not all provinces have a pension commission, so you may have to contact your Ministry of Labour or the Employment Standards Branch of your provincial government for information about pension laws and regulations. If you work for an employer under federal jurisdiction, your pension plan is regulated by the Office of the Superintendent of Financial Institutions, which operates out of the Finance Department in Ottawa.

Besides giving you information about what standards your pension plan must meet, these government pension regulators may also have booklets explaining how pension plans work and other useful information. The Pension Commission of Ontario, for instance, has an excellent booklet, written in user-friendly language, called *Understanding Your Pension Plan: A Guide for Members of Employer-Sponsored Pension Plans*, as well as a booklet called *When Your Pension Plan Winds Up* that explains what happens if your pension plan is terminated. You may be able to get similar information or booklets from your union if you belong to one.

Women and Workplace Pensions

Women's different lifetime work patterns and their family responsibilities are accommodated very well in the Canada Pension Plan, as discussed earlier. But the private workplace pension system has had much more difficulty adapting to the needs of women workers trying to accumulate pension benefits for their retirement. In many cases, women have ended up with lower pension benefits than men, even when they were in similar circumstances.

In the dark ages, just a couple of decades ago, many workplace pension plans openly discriminated against women. For one thing, women had to work longer than men before they were eligible to join the plan. Sometimes, because of the way pensions were calculated, women ended up with lower benefits than men for the same level of earnings. Sometimes, too, women had to retire earlier than men, so they didn't have as long to build up entitlement to a pension.

In some cases, although there was no overt discrimination against women workers, certain provisions that applied equally to women and men were disadvantageous for women. For example, the exclusion of part-time workers from pension plans was something that affected women much more than men because almost all part-time workers are women.

Women were similarly disadvantaged by the rules—technically known as "vesting"—specifying when an employee acquired the right to the promised pension at retirement. Up until the 1980s, the norm was generally that vesting did not occur until the employee had been a member of the plan for 10 years and had reached the age of 45. If you quit before you met these conditions, you'd get back any contributions you'd made to the pension plan, sometimes with a small amount of interest, but you wouldn't be entitled to a pension at retirement and you wouldn't benefit from anything your employer had contributed to the plan on your behalf. Although the "45 and 10" rule applied equally to women and men, women, because they have tended to change jobs more frequently than men and have sometimes left the work force to raise children, often lost out and ended up without any pension, even though they may have belonged to various workplace pension plans for most of their working life. Changes to the pension laws in the 1980s reduced the vesting period to two years in most jurisdictions, so that even if workers change jobs frequently, they are now more likely to acquire the right to a pension.

Lack of inflation indexing in private workplace pension plans is still a problem that affects women more than men because women tend to live longer. And, of course, as we have already seen with the CPP retirement pension, workplace pensions that are based on earnings give women lower benefits because women have lower average earnings.

Discriminatory provisions were largely removed from pension plans during the late 1970s and 1980s when human rights legislation made them illegal. These changes eliminated most overt forms of discrimination against women in pension plans. And changes to pension regulations, implemented by most jurisdictions in the late 1980s, have eliminated many of the other pension plan provisions that had an adverse impact on women. But these changes were generally not retroactive. That means you may still find yourself haunted by hidden or systemic discrimination because part of your pension was earned under the old regime.

For instance, the vesting period has now been shortened so that depending on which jurisdiction covers your pension plan, you'll generally be entitled to the promised benefit at retirement if you've been a member of the pension plan for two continuous years, but that applies only to benefits earned after new pension legislation came into effect. In Ontario, for example, benefits earned prior to January 1, 1987, fall under the old rules. Suppose you are now 42, you work for an employer in Ontario, and you've been a member of the workplace pension plan for the past 20 years. You're quitting tomorrow and taking a new job with another employer. The part of your pension earned up to December 31, 1986, will not be vested because although you meet the requirement of at least 10 years of service, you have not reached the age of 45 at the time you quit. If you contributed to the plan during that time, you may get your contributions back with interest when you quit. If you didn't make any contributions, you'll get nothing back. Either way, you'll lose the benefit of anything your employer contributed for you during that period before the rules were changed. But you will get a pension at retirement, based on your membership in the pension plan since January 1, 1987, because Ontario's new pension laws provide for vesting after two continuous years of plan membership.

Even with the new laws, as a woman, you may still find yourself at a disadvantage under the workplace pension system—perhaps because you work part-time or because you have taken time away from work to stay home with your children for a few years. If that's the case, you'll have to be even more disciplined in saving extra amounts on your own to make up for what you may have lost in benefits from your workplace pension plan because of your family responsibilities.

Pension Standards Laws and Women

Some of the changes in the pension benefits standards laws introduced in the 1980s were specifically designed to help women workers overcome the systemic bias they faced in the workplace pension system. There are now provisions to help part-time workers, to provide pensions for surviving spouses, and to allow pension benefits to be divided in the event of marriage breakdown (although the sharing of pension benefits at divorce generally falls under family property laws rather than under pension legislation).

Part-Time Workers

Regardless of what jurisdiction covers your pension plan, if you're a part-time worker who meets certain requirements, you must be given the option of joining the pension plan if your employer provides one for full-time workers. Pension legislation in all jurisdictions now requires that where an employer has a pension plan for full-time workers, part-time workers must be allowed to join on a prorated basis. The definition of part-time work varies from one jurisdiction to another, but, generally speaking, it is based on a minimum level of earnings, sometimes in combination with the number of hours worked. In Ontario, for example, part-time workers must be allowed to join the pension plan after 24 months' continuous service, as long as they meet either of the following two requirements: (1) the employee earned at least 35 percent of the Canada Pension Plan's Year's Maximum Pensionable Earnings (which in 1996 was $35,400) in each of the two calendar years immediately prior to membership in the plan, or (2) the employee worked at least 700 hours in each of the two calendar years immediately prior to membership in the plan. In New Brunswick, there is no requirement for a minimum number of hours worked. Part-time workers who have earned at least 35 percent of the YMPE for two consecutive years are eligible to join the pension plan if there is one.

In some cases, if a pension plan exists for full-time workers, membership for part-time workers is compulsory. But membership for part-timers is generally voluntary, and some employers will give you a choice of cash in lieu of benefits if you don't want to join. Faced with this kind of choice, it may be difficult to decide what to do. Part-time earnings are low enough to begin with, without having a percentage taken off the top to pay for a pension benefit that may seem to be very far down the road. It's always tempting to believe that you'll do better by saving on your own, but are you disciplined enough to do it? It's important that you give an honest answer to that question. If you're not sure about it, you may be better off opting for membership in the plan if you can possibly manage it. And if you take cash instead, make sure you set at least part of the money aside in your RRSP so that you will be building up some money for a pension later.

Surviving Spouses

In the past, many men who belonged to workplace pension plans failed to provide for surviving spouses because to do so would have meant accepting a lower retirement pension for themselves. Retirement pensions from workplace plans are generally designed to pay benefits only during the lifetime of the retired contributor. So, if that person wants the pension plan to continue paying a pension to a surviving spouse after his death, the amount of the retirement pension would generally be lower because it has to last longer. The pension plan, which had accumulated the funds to pay out benefits for a particular period of time, will now have to use the same accumulated funds to pay out benefits for a longer period. The amount in the fund, of course, is based on actuaries' calculations, which assume a certain life expectancy profile for plan members, based on the composition of the work force covered by the plan.

Whereas in the past a decision about whether or not to provide for a surviving spouse after the plan member's death was left up to the plan member who was generally male, the new pension laws, implemented in the late 1980s, require that surviving-spouse benefits be provided in all cases, unless both spouses waive their rights to these benefits in writing. Many women are still persuaded to sign away their right to a widow's pension because it means their husbands will receive a higher retirement pension while they are alive. But, unless some other provision has been made for your financial support after his death, this is not generally a wise thing to do. You could be left with nothing to live on after he dies. Surviving-spouse benefits will be discussed in more detail in Chapter 7.

In most pension jurisdictions, the surviving-spouse benefit must be at least 60 percent of the pension that would have been paid to the pension plan member. But again, this provision, when introduced, was not made retroactive. It applies only to benefits that commence after the relevant legislation came into effect.

Pension laws also require that a surviving-spouse benefit must continue even if the spouse remarries. In the past, whether or not your widow's pension would continue if you remarried depended on the provisions of the particular pension plan to which your spouse belonged.

Defined Benefit Pension Plans

If you work for some level of government or a large corporation, you probably have what's called a "defined benefit" pension plan. The advantage of this kind of pension plan is that once you meet the vesting requirements, you are guaranteed the promised benefit when you reach retirement. In other words, your employer or plan sponsor is on the hook to provide the benefit. That's why these pension plans are probably the best kind to have.

Calculating the Pension

It's called "defined benefit" because the pension you get at retirement is "defined"—generally in terms of your salary and years of service. The calculation may also depend on your job classification. For example, executives or management employees may have a different formula for their pensions than workers on the shop floor or in the office. You may get 1.5 percent (or some other percentage) of your average annual salary for each year of service, for example. With this particular formula, if you stay with that employer for 30 years, your pension at retirement would be 30 x 1.5%, which would be approximately 45 percent of your pre-retirement earnings.

With a workplace pension that provides a percentage of your earnings, added to the 25 percent of earnings (up to a maximum) you'll get from the CPP, figuring out how much more you'll need to save on your own to meet the income replacement goal discussed in Chapter 3 is relatively straightforward.

In this kind of defined benefit formula, the average earnings on which your retirement pension is based may be your best five or six years of earnings, or it may be your earnings in the final year before retirement. This is generally referred to as a "final average earnings formula." Other common types of formulas for calculating defined pension benefits include a "career average earnings formula," which gives you a percentage of your annual earnings for each year you participated in the pension plan—not such a good deal, since you may have to include earlier years when you had lower earnings—and a "flat-benefit formula," which gives you a flat dollar amount for each year of pensionable service. Many union-negotiated plans are flat-benefit plans, and the amount of the flat-rate benefit may be increased from time to time through the collective bargaining process.

The type of benefit formula you have will be specified in your pension plan document—the formula is not something over which you have any choice. The formula will also be outlined in the booklet you may have been given when you were hired. Knowing what the formula is will give you some idea of what kind of pension you can expect when you retire. If you don't have the information or if you can't understand it, ask your human resources department or trade union to explain it.

Inflation Protection

Even if you belong to the most generous defined benefit pension plan, the pension you eventually get may be eaten away by inflation once you retire. Check to see if your plan provides for inflation protection of your pension. If you work in the public sector, your pension will probably be automatically adjusted for inflation after you retire. But your pension may not be adjusted by the full amount of the increase in the Consumer Price Index (CPI), which is the usual measure for inflation.

If you work in the private sector, chances are your pension will not be automatically adjusted for increases in the cost of living, although many pension plans do make ad hoc inflation adjustments from time to time. It's a good idea to find out what the policy of your pension plan sponsor has been on this. But, remember, just because ad hoc inflation adjustments have been made in the past, they are not necessarily guaranteed to continue in the future.

As mentioned before, inflation adjustments are particularly important for women because we live longer. It's not for nothing that people talk about seniors living on "fixed incomes." Without indexing, your pension will remain the same for the rest of your life, regardless of how much the cost of living goes up. If you face that prospect, you'll need to take it into account in planning your retirement income. If your workplace pension seems to offer a decent benefit, but it's not indexed, you'll need to save additional funds on your own and try to build in some inflation protection for your retirement.

Integration with the CPP

Your defined benefit pension plan may be integrated with the CPP (or the QPP if you live in Quebec). That means your pension is calculated on the assumption that you'll also be getting a certain amount from the CPP when you turn 65 (or earlier if you retire early). Once you start your CPP pension, your workplace pension is reduced by the amount you're getting from the CPP. The result is that your total pension income remains the same, even after your CPP retirement pension kicks in.

Some of the proposed changes to the CPP could mean problems down the road. If CPP benefits are reduced in some way, or if you have to wait until a later age to claim a CPP pension, you may be faced with a lower retirement income than you had expected, unless your workplace pension benefits are adjusted accordingly. This is something to watch for if CPP changes go through.

How Your Defined Benefit Pension Is Funded

Your employer or pension plan sponsor is required by law to set funds aside regularly to pay the pensions the plan members will get when they retire. Pension standards laws also require that the funds are kept separately from the other assets of the plan sponsor so that your pension will be protected if the business goes under. There are also rules about what kind of investments the pension fund may make. For example, no more than 10 percent of a pension fund can be invested in the securities of any one company, and the funds must be invested prudently. The administrator of your pension plan has to establish investment policies and goals, and must review them regularly. As a plan member, you are entitled to review this information once a year. Pension regulators monitor plan sponsors to make sure they comply with these requirements.

Contributions and funding for the pensions are based on actuarial calculations, which take into account the age and gender profile of the employer's work force, as well as assumptions about what proportion of employees will reach retirement and what the life expectancy of those employees will be once they retire, together with the rate of return that the pension fund will earn.

You may or may not have to contribute to a defined benefit pension plan. In some cases, the employer or plan sponsor pays the entire cost. Because employees are not required to contribute, this type of plan is called a "non-contributory" pension plan. But remember, even if you don't contribute to the plan yourself, you pay for it indirectly because the fact that a pension plan is provided will be taken into account in setting wage levels for the employees.

Vesting and Locking In

One of the key features of a defined benefit pension plan is the point at which you become entitled to the promised benefits—technically known as "vesting." Vesting was discussed earlier in this chapter and mention was made of the fact that most pension jurisdictions now require that your pension benefits be vested after two years' continuous service. To recap, that means if you terminate your employment and you meet that condition, you'll be entitled to a pension at retirement, based on the benefit formula of your particular pension plan. If you don't meet the vesting requirements when you quit, you'll get your own contributions back with interest.

Once your benefits are vested, they are also locked in until retirement. In other words, the accumulated contributions must be used to provide a pension for you, and you won't be able to pull the money out for any other purpose. If you quit before you get to retirement age, you'll generally have a choice of options. You may be able to transfer your accumulated benefits to your new employer's pension plan, where they could be added to future contributions you make to that employer's plan so that you'll get a pension from that plan when you retire. Or you may be able to transfer the accumulated benefits to a locked-in retirement account, which operates like an RRSP, except that the funds in the plan may only be used to provide a pension. These choices are sometimes referred to as "portability" options and are described in more detail below. You may, of course, simply leave your accumulated pension benefits with the employer with whom you built up the contributions and you'll get a pension from that employer when you reach retirement age, even if you are then working somewhere else.

Like other provisions of the pension standards laws, the ones on vesting are intended as a minimum standard. Your own pension plan may allow plan members to vest sooner than the law requires. For example, some plans provide for immediate vesting, which means as soon as you join the pension plan, you acquire the right to the promised pension benefit.

The 50 Percent Solution

In the old days, when employees were contributing to a pension plan and the investments of the pension fund were doing well, employers sometimes didn't have to contribute to the plan at all because enough money was in the fund to pay all the benefits just from the employee contributions plus the earnings on them. New pension legislation changed that, too, so that now, in most jurisdictions, the plan sponsor must provide at least 50 percent of the value of the benefit earned after the new laws came into effect. That means, if you quit after your pension benefits are vested, and you have contributed more than half the value of your pension benefits to that point, you will get some money back in cash. The idea behind this is that employees who quit before they reach retirement age will get at least half of their pension paid for by their employer or plan sponsor.

Here's how it works. Suppose you worked for Acme Widget Company for six years and you decide to move on to another job with a different employer. The administrator of Acme's pension plan calculates that the pension you've accumulated to that point (technically known as the "commuted value") is worth $7,500. But your own contributions to the pension plan, plus the interest earned on your contributions, amount to $4,000. That's more than 50 percent of the value of your benefit. Since 50 percent of the value of your benefit is only $3,750, you'll get a cash refund of $250.

You Can Take It with You

But when you leave Acme Widget, you'll have a variety of portability options to choose from. These options were introduced as part of the pension reforms of the late 1980s to make sure that employees who change jobs often will still receive a pension at retirement. In other words, if you move from one employer to another, you will be able to take your pension with you.

The vested benefits you accumulated at Acme Widget may be left in Acme's plan to provide a pension for you when you reach retirement age. Another possibility is to transfer the accumulated pension to a new employer's pension plan, if that plan is willing to accept the transfer. A third option is to transfer the funds out of the Acme plan to a Locked-In Retirement Account (LIRA), where the funds can be invested to earn a return and then are converted to a pension for you at retirement. The "commuted value" of your pension, which is the amount that will be transferred, is the lump-sum payment that is estimated to be the value today of the future series of payments you would receive if you left the pension accumulated to date in the Acme plan to provide a retirement income for yourself. A fourth option might be to use the funds to purchase a "deferred life annuity." That's an arrangement whereby you'll get a monthly pension, starting at some point in the future (that's why it's called "deferred").

The introduction of portability options was particularly helpful to women workers because they have tended to be more mobile in their employment. But the changes also fit with the reality of today's workplace, where people no longer expect to work for one employer throughout their working life. Along with the rules to shorten the vesting period, portability options mean that if you join a pension plan with one employer and move on to another, you should still be able to get a pension at retirement from a combination of the various pension plans to which you belonged during your working life.

However, it's important to note that although portability rights are established in pension standards laws, they apply only to pension plan members who have vested benefits and who terminate their employment before being eligible to start receiving a retirement pension. For instance, your pension plan may provide for plan members to get an early retirement benefit at 55. If you have reached that age by the time you leave your job, you will not be able to transfer your vested benefits out of the plan to a new employer or move the commuted value of your accumulated pension into a Locked-In Retirement Account, unless your pension plan specifically allows you to do so. Instead, the pension plan must pay you a pension. You could either start your pension right away or wait until your normal retirement date. If you're thinking of quitting, and you're not sure what provisions might apply to you, ask your human resources department or benefits officer.

Locked-In Retirement Accounts

One of the most popular options for transferring vested benefits out of a registered pension plan when you terminate your employment is to transfer the accumulated pension (the "commuted value") to a locked-in retirement account (LIRA). These accounts are sometimes called locked-in RRSPs because they operate very much like an RRSP. Like RRSPs, these locked-in retirement plans are administered by financial institutions or brokers, and you choose the investments, just as you would for an RRSP. But there's one crucial difference. The funds in a locked-in retirement account may be used only to provide a pension; that is, you can't take the money out in a lump sum. To avoid confusion with regular RRSPs, these locked-in plans are now generally called Locked-In Retirement Accounts or LIRAs.

Because they contain funds from a registered pension plan, the terms and conditions of LIRAs are established by pension regulatory authorities and not by Revenue Canada. Pension standards laws specify what kinds of investments a LIRA may hold. The rules may vary slightly from one jurisdiction to another and are not necessarily the same as those allowed for regular RRSPs. In some provinces, for example, your LIRA may not invest in your own mortgage. Once your accumulated pension benefits are transferred to a LIRA, you can't make any further contributions to that particular account, although, of course, you may belong to some other workplace pension plan or be contributing to a regular RRSP.

An RRSP can be converted to a stream of income through an annuity or a Registered Retirement Income Fund (RRIF) at any age up to the end of the year in which you turn 69. However, in most jurisdictions, a LIRA may not be converted to a stream of income until the age at which you would have been entitled to a pension under the terms of the pension plan from which your funds came. In most cases, that will be 55. But as with an RRSP, you must convert your LIRA to an income stream by the end of the year in which you turn 69. The age limit used to be 71, but the 1996 federal budget changed the rules to bring the age at which RRSPs must be matured, or closed down, to age 69. (If you have a regular RRSP, you have the option at maturity of withdrawing the funds, in which case you would have to include the amount in your income and pay tax on it. With a LIRA, no such option is available. At maturity, your plan must be converted to a stream of income.) Options for converting your LIRA to a monthly pension income are not the same in all provinces.

Annuities

All pension jurisdictions, including the federal jurisdiction, allow you to convert a LIRA into an annuity. What you do is transfer the funds in your account to an insurance company, which then promises to pay you a monthly income for the rest of your life, generally with a guarantee of payment for a certain number of years. For instance, a life annuity with a 15-year guarantee means that payments will continue for the rest of your life, but you are guaranteed payments for at least 15 years. If you die only 10 years after purchasing the annuity, the balance of five years' worth of payments would be paid to your designated beneficiary.

The insurance company takes your money and invests it in order to pay your monthly benefit. So the amount of the monthly benefit you get when you purchase an annuity depends on what interest rates are at the time of your purchase. For instance, if interest rates are high at the time you purchase your annuity, monthly annuity payments will be higher than they would be if you used the same amount of money to purchase an annuity in a period when interest rates are lower.

Before deciding on the amount of your monthly benefit, the insurance company also makes an assessment of how long it believes it will have to go on paying benefits to you—in other words, how long the company expects you will live. Because women live longer than men, women get lower monthly annuity benefits than men for the same original lump sum. That's why you see different male and female rates quoted in annuity tables, which are issued by some financial institutions or advisers, and which show what monthly annuity benefits can be purchased with various lump sums at different ages.

Although insurance companies claim that such differentiation is justified, during the debate on pension reform in the early 1980s, many people argued that this kind of discrimination against women should not be permitted. As a result, some pension jurisdictions adopted "unisex mortality tables." Insurance companies consult mortality tables, which show life expectancy of women and men at different ages, to determine the amount of the annuity benefit the company will be able to pay to people who want to purchase an annuity. Generally, there are separate tables for women and men. A "unisex mortality table" combines male and female life expectancies in one table to determine what monthly benefits will be payable for various lump sums used to purchase pensions or annuities.

Life Income Funds

All pension jurisdictions also allow you the alternative of converting your LIRA to a Life Income Fund (LIF). This operates like a Registered Retirement Income Fund (RRIF), which is described in

Chapter 6. In the case of a LIF, there is a minimum annual withdrawal and a maximum amount you may withdraw each year; however, with a RRIF, there is only a minimum annual withdrawal amount and no maximum limit. The objective of these rules is to make sure the money in your LIF won't run out before you do. In other words, your LIF will pay you a pension for the rest of your life. Another twist is that funds in a LIF must be converted to an annuity by the end of the year in which you reach the age of 80. The same financial institutions and brokers selling RRIFs also offer LIFs, and many of these companies and brokers have helpful booklets that explain in more detail how these plans work.

In Alberta and Saskatchewan, you also have the option of converting your LIRA to a Locked-in Retirement Income Fund (LRIF). Essentially, this is the same as a LIF, except that you don't have to convert it to an annuity at the age of 80. In effect, the LRIF continues for the rest of your life.

Your employer or trade union should be able to give you more details about what options you have in your province or pension jurisdiction, or you may want to contact your provincial Pension Commission or Ministry of Labour.

Your Right to Information

Pension laws generally require the sponsor of your pension plan to give you an annual statement with information about your own pension entitlement. The statement must tell you the amount of the pension you've accumulated so far and the amounts you contributed in the past year and since you became a member of the plan. Your annual statement will also include information about the date on which you are expected to retire—technically referred to as your "normal retirement date"—as well as indicating the person you have designated as your beneficiary.

The administrator of your pension plan is also required by law to give you a written explanation of the provisions of the pension plan, as well as a written explanation of any changes to the plan that will affect you. Pension standards laws also require your plan sponsor to give you notice if the plan is going to be wound up.

Accommodating Family Responsibilities

Workplace pension plans generally don't do a very good job of accommodating women's family responsibilities. Some pension plans allow employees to buy back previous service when they return from an extended leave period. But the requirements may be particularly onerous for women. If you work for the federal government, for example, you may take up to five years' unpaid leave for care and nurturing of a pre-school child. But since participation in the federal public service pension plan is mandatory, when you return to work, you have to make up the pension plan contributions missed while you were away. In the period immediately after you come back from leave, you have to pay your own current service contributions to the pension plan, plus both your own and your employer's contributions for the period you were away. Having to pay triple contributions to the pension plan at a time when you also face additional costs for child care is prohibitively expensive for most people. In fact, some women decide not to return to the public service after taking this kind of parental leave because they can't afford to "buy back" their pensionable service. Recent changes to the federal pension plan have made these conditions a bit more flexible and have given women more time to make up the lost contributions, but it's still a heavy cost. Periods outside the work force without earnings, of course, make it even more difficult to compensate with your own savings for the gap in your pension plan coverage. In fact, without an earned income, you're not allowed to contribute to an RRSP—even if you could somehow find the money.

Buying back past service may also be an option if you've been on some other kind of leave—such as educational leave—or if you've had a period of time working for another employer before returning to the employer you worked for originally. The advantage of doing this is that by making up any gaps in your contribution record, you become entitled both to a full benefit at retirement and to additional benefits provided by the pension plan, such as those for a surviving spouse or dependent children of deceased contributors. Some pension plans allow a buyback of past service through a lump-sum purchase or through regular monthly payments. And if you haven't finished making the monthly payments by the time you retire, they can be deducted monthly from your pension cheque. If you're interested in these options, you should be able to get details from your employer or pension plan sponsor.

If you're considering buying back past service, you'll also need to weigh the cost of doing so against the kind of return you might be able to get by investing the money in your RRSP instead—assuming you have enough contribution room to be able to do that. Often, your benefits officer or human resources department can help you decide by doing this kind of calculation for you.

Defined Contribution Pension Plans

Although most workplace pension plans are defined benefit plans, about 9 percent of Canadian workers who belong to workplace pension plans are members of defined contribution plans. These plans are popular with smaller employers because defined contribution plans are less costly to operate and the employer does not have to guarantee any particular benefit to the employee at retirement. That, of course, is the disadvantage of these plans for you as an employee. It's often hard to predict just what kind of pension you'll get from a defined contribution plan.

As the name implies, a "defined contribution" pension plan is one in which only the contribution is specified. Both employer and employee—or sometimes just the employer—contribute a percentage of the employee's earnings to a fund, and whatever is in the fund when the employee is ready to retire is used to buy the pension. That's why these plans are also known as "money purchase" plans, reflecting the fact that the money in the fund when you retire is used to purchase a pension benefit. Like defined benefit pension plans, a defined contribution plan where employees are not required to contribute is also called a "non-contributory" plan.

If your workplace pension plan is a money purchase plan, effectively you are bearing the entire risk of providing a pension for your retirement. Your employer or plan sponsor does not promise you any particular pension benefit in relation to your earnings or years of service. The investment performance of your fund will largely determine the amount available to purchase your pension. And, just like an annuity, the amount of the pension you get when you're ready to retire will depend largely on what interest rates are doing at that time. You may even find that a colleague with exactly the same work history and earnings as you, and the same amount in her retirement fund, ends up with a bigger pension because she retired when interest rates were high, and you retired a few months later when interest rates had dropped. Or you may retire at the same time as a male colleague with the same amount in your fund, but you get a lower benefit because you're a woman. This is because, as explained earlier, insurance companies that provide pension annuities say that because you will likely live longer than your male colleague, the insurance company will have to go on paying your benefit for a longer period of time, and therefore will have to offer you a lower monthly amount than a male retiree with the same lump sum.

Some employers decide to convert their defined benefit pension plans to a defined contribution plan so that they no longer have to guarantee a specific pension when the employee retires. And some companies say that having to comply with the pension standards laws is too onerous and costly. Converting a defined benefit pension plan to a defined contribution plan shifts the entire risk and responsibility for providing the pension on to you. Generally, you will have to be responsible for making the investment decisions, and it will be your problem if your fund doesn't do very well or if interest rates are low when you have to purchase your pension. This gets your employer off the hook.

If you belong to a defined benefit plan and your employer decides to convert it to a defined contribution plan, the law requires that you be notified. But it may not be easy to figure out what is going on or what it means to your future financial security. One magazine writer was called to a meeting of workers in her office, where their employer told them about a new, improved pension plan that was to be implemented. "This will be much better for you," the employees were told. "You'll be able to choose what you want to invest in, and the funds will be under your control. You'll probably get a much better pension than you would have had under our current pension plan." After this glowing account, significant for its lack of detail, the employees were asked if they had any questions. No one did. What the employees didn't understand was that their defined benefit pension plan, which guaranteed them a pension that was a percentage of their earnings for each year of service, was being converted to a defined contribution plan that no longer guaranteed any benefits related to their earnings or years of service.

More and more employers also seem to be converting their defined benefit pension plans to group RRSPs as a cost-saving measure. While these plan conversions get employers off the hook as far as guaranteeing a pension goes, for employees, group RRSPs, described later, have all the disadvantages of money purchase plans.

Investing Your Defined Contributions

Many defined contribution plans give employees a choice of investments for their funds. Sometimes you get to choose from a selection of specially managed funds, something like special mutual funds, and sometimes it's a choice of the same kinds of investments you might select for your RRSP. You may be offered stocks, bonds, balanced funds, fixed income funds, or Guaranteed Investment Certificates (GICs). In all likelihood, you'll be given the opportunity to select a combination of these investments for your personal pension fund.

The problem is, of course, that most employees are not experienced investors and don't have the background needed to make good choices or to put together a portfolio of investments that suit their own particular needs. A professional fund manager—the kind of person who manages the pension fund investments for employers with defined benefit pension plans—is skilled at managing investments, balancing security with risk and the need for decent returns, and setting up a diversified portfolio, and is used to investing for the long term to generate the money needed to pay the promised benefits when the employees retire. All the surveys show that when people are asked to manage their own funds, they tend to be very conservative investors; they panic if the market goes down, and they don't think long-term. The result, of course, is that they generally end up with much lower pensions than they might have had if the same funds had been managed by a professional fund manager. Of course, there are exceptions, but they're rare.

If you're in a defined contribution pension plan and you're faced with having to choose investments for your fund, that may seem like a bewildering prospect. One solution is to do some homework. Ask around, take an investing course, read up on investing, and get as much information as you can. Your future financial security is at stake here. Here are a few key rules you should consider:

- You need a balanced, diversified portfolio. Investing all your funds in Guaranteed Investment Certificates (GICs) may be super-safe, but they won't give you the kind of return you'll need to build up a decent pension for your retirement, especially in a time of very low interest rates. You'd be surprised, though, how many people do invest all their funds in GICs. Your portfolio should have at least some stocks or "equities" in it to generate a better return over the long term. If investing in the stock market makes you nervous, consider a balance of good quality stocks and bonds, along with other types of investments, such as GICs, for your fund.
- Remember, you're investing for the long term. Your objective is to get a steady, decent rate of return. While you need to watch your plan on an ongoing basis, you shouldn't be tempted to switch your investments if the market goes up or down. Your defined contribution pension plan may allow you the option of changing your investment mix every six months, or even more often. But if you've chosen your portfolio well to begin with, you shouldn't need to keep switching your investments around.
- As a member of a defined contribution pension plan, you may get bombarded with investment information, some of which may sound authoritative and persuasive. But remember, much of this "information" is directed at getting you to buy or generate commissions for someone. Think carefully before you are persuaded.
- Above all, you need to be comfortable with your investments. That's the cardinal rule of any investment strategy, whether for your pension plan, your RRSP, or a regular investment portfolio. Your choice of investments must reflect the degree of comfort you have with taking risks—what the experts call your "risk tolerance."

Hybrid Plans and Multi-Employer Plans

Not all workplace pension plans fit neatly into the categories of defined benefit or defined contribution. Some plans are a combination of both types of plan, and these are often called "hybrid" plans. If your pension plan seems to be a hybrid plan, with features of both defined benefit and defined contribution, you may want to ask your benefits officer or human resources department to explain just what kind of pension you can expect to get at retirement and how much of that is guaranteed as a benefit in relation to your earnings or years of service.

Perhaps you are a member of a multi-employer pension plan, which is a pension plan set up for employees of two or more employers. Multi-employer plans are often negotiated by trade unions for workers in a particular sector—for example, hospital employees. Contributions made to a multi-employer pension plan will be determined by your service with one or more of the employers included in the plan. And your plan may be either defined benefit or defined contribution.

Multi-employer pension plans that are defined benefit plans differ from other kinds of defined benefit plans. Different pension standards laws may apply, and the pension benefits are not necessarily guaranteed. This is because the employer's contribution to the pension plan, generally negotiated through collective bargaining and set out in the collective agreement, is limited to a fixed amount—for example, a number of cents per hour of time worked. If the funds contributed to the plan by the employer are not enough to pay the promised pension benefits, the pension payable at retirement may have to be reduced.

If you belong to a multi-employer pension plan, your union should be able to give you more details about these provisions and how they might affect you.

Deferred Profit-Sharing Plans

It's possible your employer has set up a Deferred Profit-Sharing Plan (DPSP) for employees. Effectively, these plans are retirement savings plans to which an employer makes contributions from the profits of the business. There's no obligation for the employer to make contributions if there are no profits during the year. Employee contributions to a Deferred Profit-Sharing Plan are now prohibited, although they used to be permitted until a few years ago. These plans may form part of your retirement savings package at work, and any contribution made to a DPSP by your employer will be factored into your pension adjustment (discussed later) for tax purposes.

There is a limit on the amount an employer may contribute to a DPSP, and it is equivalent to about half of the contribution limit for a defined contribution pension plan. A DPSP must be registered with Revenue Canada, and vesting—in this case, obtaining your right to your employer's contributions—must occur after no more than two years of plan membership. But a DPSP may let you withdraw some or all of your vested benefits at any time, while you are still employed by your employer. You may also receive the money in your DPSP if you leave the employer. On maturity of a DPSP, which must happen by the end of the year you turn 69, the money in the plan may be paid out in either a cash lump sum or in equal instalments over a period of up to 10 years, or used to purchase an annuity. Payments out of a DPSP are taxable. You will have to include them in your income as you receive them—whether as a lump sum or as periodic annuity payments. However, a lump-sum entitlement from a DPSP may be transferred tax-free to your RRSP.

Group RRSPs

The least costly option for employers who want to assist their employees in saving for retirement is to set up a group RRSP. Often an employer does not contribute to a group RRSP, but sets it up simply as a convenience for employees. The group plan is usually administered by a financial institution or mutual fund, and the employer may pay the administration fees. As the name implies, a group RRSP is really a program of individual Registered Retirement Savings Plans, established for employees as a group. Your contribution to a group RRSP will be deducted from your pay and must fall within your regular RRSP contribution limit (described in Chapter 6). If your employer also contributes to the plan for you, it will be considered a taxable benefit to you for tax purposes.

As noted earlier, group RRSPs are not really "pension plans." They don't have to be registered with Revenue Canada in the way that defined benefit or money purchase pension plans must, nor do they have to meet the requirements of provincial and federal pension regulations.

Like many defined contribution plans, group RRSPs usually allow you to choose the investments for your plan. That raises the same problems as investment decisions you may have to make for a defined contribution pension plan (which was discussed earlier). For the same reasons, group RRSPs often provide lower benefits than a comparable defined benefit pension plan. But more and more employees who have any kind of workplace pension arrangement are finding themselves members of group RRSPs. The Canadian Life and Health Association estimated that in the five-year period between 1986 and 1991 alone, membership in group RRSPs increased by more than 150 percent.

While a group RRSP is not subject to pension laws, your employer may not allow you to withdraw funds from your plan until retirement. However, these restrictions cannot be maintained if you leave the company. In that case, the RRSP goes with you and becomes just like any other RRSP you may have. The funds are not locked in and you will then be able to withdraw money from the plan if you wish.

Workplace Pensions and Your Income Tax

Revenue Canada's rules for registered pension plans limit the maximum pension benefit that can be accumulated through a defined benefit plan to $1,722 for each year of service. The limits are designed to allow individuals to accumulate a tax-assisted retirement pension equivalent to 70 percent of their pre-retirement annual earnings up to an earnings limit of 2½ times the average wage, or about $86,000 a year. That's almost three times the average earnings of a woman who works full-time for a full year. And it's in sharp contrast to the limits on the CPP, which allows people to accumulate a pension of only 25 percent of earnings up to the average wage, which in 1996 was expected to be about $35,400.

Any contributions you are required to make to a defined benefit workplace pension plan may be deducted for tax purposes to a maximum of $3,500 in each taxation year. You are also allowed an additional tax deduction of up to $3,500 a year for amounts you have to pay to buy back past pensionable service, described earlier in this chapter. The amount you contributed during the year for current pensionable service will be shown in box 20 of the T4 slip your employer sends you early in the year, or on your union dues receipt. Any contributions made to buy back past pensionable service will be shown in box 20 of your T4 slip or box 32 of your T4A slip.

Contributions to defined contribution pension plans are limited to the lesser of 18 percent of the employee's compensation for the particular calendar year and a maximum dollar amount, which for 1996 was $13,500. The amount is frozen until 2004, when it increases to $14,500. In 2005, it is scheduled to increase to $15,500, and it will be indexed to the average wage after that. Since the government sometimes changes these limits or postpones scheduled increases, you may want to check with your local taxation office to verify the current contribution limit. Contributions you make to a defined contribution pension plan will also be shown on your T4 slip, so you can deduct them, for tax purposes.

The Pension Adjustment

As well as showing what amounts you may deduct for pension plan contributions when you file your income tax return, if you belong to a workplace pension plan, your T4 slip will also indicate a pension adjustment (PA) in box 52, or this amount may appear in box 34 of your T4A slip. If you worked for more than one employer during the year and both employers had a pension plan, you may have more than one PA.

The concept of a PA was introduced a few years ago to level the playing field between taxpayers who belong to registered pension plans and those who save for retirement through RRSPs. Your PA determines whether you will also be able to contribute to an RRSP, but the PA doesn't affect your income. Before the rules changed, if you belonged to a non-contributory pension plan (that is, a pension plan to which you did not contribute), you were allowed to contribute to a regular RRSP as well, up to certain maximum amounts. Members of contributory pension plans (that is, plans to which employees had to contribute) did not have the same opportunity. The PA takes into account pension benefits accumulated in your workplace pension plan—whether that's a defined benefit or defined contribution plan—even if you contribute nothing to the plan yourself. The idea is that if you're building up a pension through your workplace pension plan, you shouldn't also be able to contribute large additional amounts to an RRSP. The tax assistance for retirement savings is now roughly equivalent, whether a person saves through a defined benefit plan, a defined contribution plan, or an RRSP.

The PA reflects the total of your pension credits accrued for the year under the terms of your workplace pension plan or Deferred Profit-Sharing Plan (DPSP) if you participate in such a plan. It is your employer's responsibility to calculate your PA and to inform you of the amount. You then use the PA to help figure out if you also have room to contribute to an RRSP. Your RRSP contribution room is based on 18 percent of your earned income from the previous year, up to a maximum amount, minus your PA for the previous year.

If you're buying back past pensionable service, you may also have a Past Service Pension Adjustment (PSPA), which must also be deducted from the 18 percent of your previous year's earned income to figure out your allowable RRSP contribution limit. You'll find a detailed description of these calculations, along with a form for doing them, in a free booklet from Revenue Canada called *RRSP and Other Registered Plans for Retirement*, which you can get from your local taxation office.

CHAPTER 6

REGISTERED RETIREMENT SAVINGS PLANS

One thing is certain about planning for retirement these days: the more you can save for yourself, the better off you'll be. With government programs being cut or scaled back, and coverage of workplace pension plans declining, people will have to count on their own savings to provide much more of their income in retirement. Luckily, the government gives you lots of help to save on your own. You can contribute up to 18 percent of your income to a Registered Retirement Savings Plan (RRSP) and you'll be able to claim a tax deduction for the entire amount—to a limit of $13,500 a year.

That sounds like a lot, until you stop and think about it. If you're the typical woman, working full-time for most of the year, your total earnings are only $27,000 a year. Being able to set aside 18 percent of that in an RRSP is probably out of the question. Indeed, many women don't take advantage of RRSPs, no doubt because they can't afford to. You only have to look at the numbers. The latest information shows that only 26 percent of women who were over 25 and didn't have a workplace pension plan were contributing to an RRSP instead.

What about the other 74 percent? They may be putting money aside once in a while, but few seem to be doing so on a regular basis. Statistics Canada says that in the three-year period from 1991 to

1993, only 19 percent of women aged 25 to 64 who were entitled to contribute to an RRSP actually contributed in every one of those three years. A staggering 61 percent who were entitled to contribute to an RRSP didn't do so in any of the three years.

Not much information about the amounts people have accumulated in their RRSPs is available. But we do know that more and more people are cashing in their savings when they fall on hard times. That was particularly true during the recession of the early 1990s, when there was a surge in the number of people cashing in their RRSPs before the age of 65. While some of them may have been older workers taking early retirement, more than half were under the age of 45, and most had no employment income and were not receiving unemployment insurance benefits.

And how many women do you know who have cashed in their RRSPs to finance their maternity leave? You may even have done it yourself, and now you're faced with making up the lost savings before you retire. So you have plenty of time to do it, so what's the problem? The difficulty is that it may take longer than you think. And in the meantime, you've lost the benefit of tax-free compounding of interest, which is such an attractive feature of RRSPs.

Making the most of your RRSP is vital to your financial security in retirement. But you need to be realistic about it too. Don't overestimate what you can afford to save on your own. Consider carefully how much money you'll need in order to provide yourself with a decent income in retirement and whether or not it's realistic to count on doing most of the saving through your RRSP. (Have another look at Chapter 3 if you still need convincing.)

Take Kathleen. She's 45 years old, married with two children aged nine and twelve, works part-time, and earns about $20,000 a year. Her husband has a pension plan at work, so she does have something to fall back on—as long as her marriage lasts. When I spoke to her, she had $45,000 in her RRSP. By the time she retires in 20 years, she expects those funds will have grown to $400,000. She believes she will be able to live off these investments when she retires. Is that realistic, or is Kathleen in for a rude shock?

We can do the calculations, using the worksheets from Chapter 3. If Kathleen can earn an average rate of return of 8 percent a year on her existing RRSP, her $45,000 will have increased to almost $210,000 by the time she's ready to retire—20 years from now—even if she doesn't make any more contributions. That's what financial planners call "the power of compound interest." But that's assuming Kathleen has the willpower to let her fund build up over the years and that she doesn't have to dip into her savings during that time. This also assumes that the return she earns on her RRSP investments will average 8 percent a year for the next 20 years. Whether or not she'll be able to achieve that will depend on how her fund is invested. But if she doesn't achieve that 8 percent average, and her fund earns an average of 6 percent a year, let's say, she'll have only $144,000 in her RRSP by the time she wants to retire.

Then there's the question of the shortfall. If Kathleen wants a fund of $400,000 when she's 65, even if her current $45,000 does earn an average 8 percent rate of return resulting in almost $210,000 in 20 years' time, she'll have to find another $190,000 from somewhere else to meet her goal. Assuming the same average annual rate of return of 8 percent on her savings, she will have to save almost $4,200 a year to reach her retirement fund goal. And what if she can earn only an average of 6 percent a year on her RRSP? She would have to add another $256,000 before turning 65 to reach her goal of $400,000. That would mean saving almost $7,000 a year for the next 20 years, assuming the same 6 percent average annual rate of return on her savings. But she earns only $20,000 a year from her part-time job. That means she won't be able to save enough through her RRSP because her maximum contribution is 18 percent of her earnings, or about $3,600, based on what she's making right now.

Of course, Kathleen could get a full-time job and perhaps save more. But it doesn't look as if she has really thought this through. Besides, the fund of $400,000 that she hopes for would provide her with an annual income of $34,500 in today's dollars, which is more than she currently makes from her job. Maybe that's not a realistic goal. It's probably far more than she needs, especially considering she'll have other sources of retirement income, such as public programs and maybe a share in her husband's pension. And even if we give her the benefit of the doubt, whether she can make it depends on: getting that average 8 percent annual rate of return, being really disciplined about saving the necessary amount every year, and not dipping into her savings at all for 20 years.

It's a cautionary tale that may seem discouraging. But the moral of the story is to do your homework, and understand both the benefits and the limitations of RRSPs.

What Is an RRSP?

Registered Retirement Savings Plans made their appearance in Canada in 1957 when the Income Tax Act was amended to allow individuals to make deposits into personal retirement savings plans and to get the same tax advantages that people who belonged to workplace pension plans were already getting. The rest, as they say, is history. Promoting, selling, writing, and talking about RRSPs has now become a huge part of the business of financial institutions and the financial media. Consumers are bombarded with a bewildering avalanche of information about RRSPs—especially as the annual deadline for contributions approaches each spring.

The basic idea of an RRSP is that you contribute to your plan during your working life, claiming a tax deduction for the amount of your contribution. Your plan earns interest, dividends, or capital gains, just like regular investments outside the RRSP, with the exception that the funds in the RRSP remain sheltered and not subject to tax. When you start to withdraw the money from your RRSP, you pay tax on the withdrawn amounts—both on the amounts you contributed and the interest those amounts have earned. (Since you deducted the full amount of your RRSP contribution when you put the money into your plan, of course, this will be the only time this income has been taxed.)

In spite of the fact that we call these plans "retirement savings plans," there's nothing to stop you from taking out your money at any time and using it for whatever you like. However, whatever you take out of the plan—whether it's a lump sum or regular monthly payments after you've converted your RRSP to an annuity, for instance—has to be included in your income in the year you make the withdrawal, and you'll have to pay tax on it. Of course, if you take the money out in a year when you have no other income—when you're on maternity leave, for example—you probably won't have much tax to pay. That's why it's so tempting to use your RRSP in this way. For example, if you took $6,000 out of your RRSP in a year when you had no other income, you likely wouldn't pay any tax on the money at all because of basic personal income tax exemptions that everyone is allowed to claim. But if you took $6,000 out in a year when you also earned $30,000 in your job, you'd have to pay something like $2,400 in tax on your withdrawal, depending on which province you live in.

Because your contribution to an RRSP is deducted from your income before you estimate the income tax you owe, the higher your income, the higher the tax break you'll get. For instance, if you contribute $1,000 to an RRSP and you're in a 50 percent tax bracket (that is, your taxable income is about $60,000 or more), you would get a tax refund of $500, or 50 percent of $1,000. The same $1,000 contribution if you're in a 26 percent tax bracket (that is, your taxable income is about $28,000) would generate a tax refund of only $260.

Not only do higher-income earners get bigger tax breaks than lower-income earners for the same RRSP contribution, but higher-income earners are also allowed to contribute more than lower-income earners to an RRSP because the contribution is based on a percentage of income.

The rules for RRSPs are set out in the Income Tax Act, which specifies such issues as how much you may contribute, how you deduct it from your income for tax purposes, and what your plan may invest in.

Your Contribution Limit

The amount you may contribute to an RRSP—sometimes also called your "deduction limit" or your "contribution room" or your "contribution limit" is 18 percent of your earned income from the previous year, up to a maximum dollar limit. For 1996 through to the year 2003, the maximum dollar limit is $13,500. The government plans to raise that limit to $14,500 in 2004 and to $15,500 in 2005—although nothing is ever carved in stone. Many people have urged that these limits be scaled back because of the huge cost of this program to the government in lost tax revenues and also because it gives the biggest benefits to those with the highest incomes. The federal government itself estimates it loses about $15 billion a year because of the tax deductions for contributions to workplace pension plans and RRSPs. It's quite possible the dollar limits may be reduced or that planned increases in limits may be postponed in the future. But it's probably not something most women need to worry about. To make a maximum contribution of $15,500, which will be the contribution limit when the system is fully phased in, you would need an earned income of roughly $86,000 a year, which is 3½ times the average annual earnings of a woman who works full-time. To reach the current top contribution limit of $13,500, you'd need an earned income of $75,000, and few women—or even men, for that matter—reach those dizzying heights. Statistics Canada's data show only 2 percent of female wage earners have earnings above $60,000. About 11 percent of male workers earn $60,000 or more a year.

Defining Your Earned Income

To figure out how much you're entitled to contribute to an RRSP, you need to list your earned income. That's basically your earnings, but it may include other types of income too. However, it does not include investment income.

You'll find a handy chart for calculating your RRSP deduction limit in the free booklet, mentioned previously in Chapter 5, called *RRSP and Other Registered Plans for Retirement*. You can get the booklet from your local taxation office, which is listed in the phone book under Government of Canada, Revenue Canada Tax Services. Revenue Canada also runs the tax information phone system, known as TIPs, where you can get information by phone on RRSP limits and other features of these plans. That number is also listed in the phone book under Revenue Canada.

Most of the items needed to calculate your earned income can be read off your income tax return. First, take your employment earnings, deduct any union or professional dues, then add net income from any business you may have, any disability payments you received from the CPP or QPP, royalty income if you have received any, net rental income, and any child support or maintenance payments you received. The total is the amount on which your RRSP contribution will be based. If you paid child support or maintenance to anyone, those payments must be deducted from your earnings to determine the amount on which your RRSP contribution limit will be based. The calculation for people paying or receiving child support will change when the government introduces new rules on the fair treatment of child support, promised in the 1996 budget.

Timing Your Contribution

Once you've figured out how much you're entitled to contribute to an RRSP, you can make your contribution any time during the year and during the first 60 days of the following year. For the 1996 taxation year, for example, you can contribute to your RRSP up to March 1, 1997. Occasionally, the government extends the deadline by a day or two, if the final date falls on a weekend. And in leap years, the deadline is generally February 29.

In recognition of the overwhelming human tendency to leave everything until the last minute, many financial institutions stay open late—sometimes until midnight—on RRSP deadline day. But the worst possible way to make your RRSP contribution is to rush down to the bank with 15 minutes to spare and grab whatever plan happens to be the flavour of the month. For one thing, the plan may not be suited to your needs. But worse still, by leaving it until the last minute, you've lost the benefit of more than a whole year's worth of tax-free compounding that could have been yours if you'd made the contribution at the beginning of the previous year.

If you can't come up with a lump sum to make your RRSP contribution early, consider setting up a regular monthly transfer from your bank account to your RRSP. Most financial institutions will be only too happy to arrange it. And if you're investing in a mutual fund (which will be discussed later) you can set up a pre-authorized payment plan and make your RRSP contribution relatively painlessly each month.

Borrowing to Invest in Your RRSP

But what if you didn't plan ahead? What if you're now right down to the wire and you just can't come up with the funds to make even a minimal contribution to your RRSP? Consider borrowing to make your contribution. Interest on money borrowed to invest is generally tax-deductible, but that does not apply to money borrowed to invest in an RRSP. However, most financial institutions will happily lend you money to invest in an RRSP—especially if you invest at the same financial institution where you borrowed the money. And there are advantages to you as well. The biggest advantage, of course, is that you will be able to get some money into your RRSP where it can give a boost to your retirement savings. But your investment in the RRSP will generate a tax refund, which can be used to pay off a chunk of the loan.

For example, suppose you earn about $28,000 a year and you live in Nova Scotia. Your marginal tax rate, or the rate at which an additional dollar of earnings would be taxed, would be 26 percent. (Rates vary slightly from one province to another because provincial income tax rates differ.) Any amount deducted from your income for tax purposes such as an RRSP contribution would produce a tax rebate of 26 percent too. In other words, if you contributed $2,000 to your RRSP, you'd get 26 percent of $2,000 (or $520) back when you file your tax return. If you had borrowed the $2,000 to make your contribution, you could use the refund to pay back part of the loan and you'd be left with a debt of just $1,480, plus interest. Financial institutions usually require RRSP loans to be paid back over a one-year period. But with the tax refund and the low rates of interest now being charged, that shouldn't be too difficult to do.

Deducting Your Contribution

Once you've figured out your contribution limit and deposited the funds in your RRSP, you can claim the amount as a deduction from your income when you file your income tax return. The confusing thing is that while you must have earned income to be entitled to contribute to an RRSP, you don't need earned income to be able to deduct the contribution once you've made it. That's because your RRSP contribution is deducted from your total income. As well, because your RRSP contribution limit is based on your earned income for the previous year, you may be entitled to make an RRSP contribution in a year when you have no earnings—for instance, if you take a leave of absence from work or in the first year after you retire.

Suppose you retire in June 1997. Since you had earned income in 1996, you will be able to make an RRSP contribution for the 1997 tax year. You will even be able to contribute for the 1998 tax year, based on your earned income for the first six months of 1997. Your contributions for 1997 and 1998 can be deducted from your total income from all sources in those years, including pension income and investment income.

Carry-Forwards, PAs, and Other Complications

What if you're entitled to contribute to an RRSP but you don't have the money to make the contribution this year? You're allowed to carry the unused contribution room forward to use in a subsequent year. Let's suppose your contribution limit for 1996 was $6,000, but you contributed only $2,000 to your RRSP for that tax year. And let's assume in 1997, your contribution limit is $7,000. The $4,000 you didn't use in 1996 will be added to the $7,000 of new room that becomes available in 1997, giving you a contribution limit of $11,000 for the 1997 tax year.

There used to be a limit of seven years for the carry-forward of unused RRSP contribution room. But in 1996, the federal government abolished the limit. Now, unused RRSP contribution room accumulated since 1991 may be carried forward indefinitely. The Finance Minister's 1996 budget speech pointed out that "many people go through lengthy periods—early in their careers or when they are raising children—when they are unable to set significant amounts aside for their retirement." He claimed the abolition of the seven-year limit would allow people to use their accumulated contribution room in years when they are able to save. It sounds like something that would be especially helpful to women. The trouble is that the more unused contribution room you build up, the less likely it is you'll be able to come up with the money you need to use the built-up contribution room—unless, of course, you come into an inheritance or you win the lottery. Even with a contribution limit of just $3,000 a year, carrying it forward for five years while you stay home with the kids, for example, will mean you'll have to come up with a lump sum of $15,000 if you want to use it up.

However, by the end of 1996, some financial institutions were beginning to develop special loans to help customers take advantage of large amounts of RRSP contribution room they had built up because of the carry-forward provisions. In November 1996, for example, the Bank of Nova Scotia introduced its "RRSP Catch-Up Loan," by which eligible customers can borrow up to $50,000 at a very low rate of interest to invest in the bank's RRSPs. Slightly higher rates of interest were charged if you used the loan to invest in RRSPs at another financial institution. The loan could be paid off ("amortized") over a 10-year period. Normally, RRSP loans have to be paid off in one year.

Pension Adjustments and Your Contribution Limit

If you belong to a workplace pension plan, even if you don't have to contribute anything to the plan, your ability to contribute to an RRSP as well will be restricted. That's because you'll have a pension adjustment (PA). As explained in Chapter 5, the PA represents the amount of pension you have accumulated in your workplace pension plan during the year. It will be shown in box 52 of the T4 slip your employer sends you each year for you to use when you fill out your income tax return. If you have a PA, it must be deducted from the 18 percent of your earned income you're limited to, as discussed above, to determine how much you'll be allowed to contribute to your RRSP.

If you're buying back past pensionable service, as explained earlier, you may have a past service pension adjustment (PSPA), which also has to be deducted from the 18 percent of your earned income before you can determine your RRSP contribution room. The PSPA will be shown on your T4 slip too.

If all this sounds horribly complicated, don't despair. Revenue Canada does the calculation for you. When you get your assessment notice, which is Revenue Canada's sign-off on your tax return, sent to you a few months after you file your return, you'll see a special section, generally at the bottom of the second page, headed "Registered Retirement Savings Plan Deduction Limit Statement." In this section, you'll find a statement showing: (1) your deduction limit for the current tax year, (2) that limit minus the amount you claimed for the year, (3) the resulting amount plus the amount you're entitled to contribute for the next year, and (4) the resulting amount minus any PAs or PSPAs. The grand total shows the amount you may claim as an RRSP deduction for the coming year, including amounts carried forward from past years.

The only problem is that, depending on when you file your tax return, you may not get your assessment notice until about the middle of the year. That could scupper any good intentions you may have had about contributing to your RRSP early in the year, since you may not know exactly how much you're entitled to contribute until you get the assessment notice. Although it's challenging, you can, in fact, do the calculations yourself—as explained above—without waiting for the notice. And, of course, you can always start putting at least some money into your plan early in the year, even if you can't figure out your limit exactly.

Overcontributions

Revenue Canada also recognizes that, in this rather complicated system, people may make mistakes and inadvertently contribute too much to their RRSPs. So it allows you to make an overcontribution of up to $2,000 without penalty. By definition, an overcontribution is an amount you contributed to your RRSP that is over and above the amount you were allowed to contribute, so you can't claim it as a deduction. At any point in time, as long as the amount doesn't exceed $2,000 you'll be all right. But if you go over the limit, you'll be penalized. You'll be charged a tax of 1 percent a month for each month your total overcontributions were above your limit. The penalty tax must be paid no later than 90 days after the end of the year in which the excess overcontribution exists.

To make matters more complicated, the government announced changes in the overcontribution rules in the 1995 budget, to start at the beginning of 1996. Before that, the overcontribution limit was $8,000. If you had an overcontribution in your RRSP on the day before the budget was presented, you won't be penalized if it was within the old $8,000 limit. But you will have to use it up as new RRSP contribution room becomes available. For instance, suppose you had an $8,000 overcontribution that had been in your RRSP since early 1995, and in 1996, your RRSP contribution limit was $10,000. Your contribution room must first be used to bring your overcontribution down to the $2,000 limit. You will need $6,000 to do that ($8,000 minus $2,000 = $6,000). That leaves a balance of only $4,000, which you may contribute to your RRSP (your $10,000 contribution room minus the $6,000 you need to cover the excess overcontribution already in your plan).

Although technically the overcontribution limit is intended to cover inadvertent overcontributions to an RRSP, some financial advisers suggest deliberate overcontributions are a good idea. Even if you can't deduct the amount of your overcontribution, the money can earn interest tax-free, and you can deduct it later as more contribution room becomes available. There's some truth in this. But if you've got a $2,000 overcontribution in your plan already, and you then make a miscalculation and put even more in, you're leaving yourself open to the stiff penalty for excess overcontributions. There is a safety valve available, though. If you contribute too much to your plan by mistake, you can take it out again without penalty, as long as you withdraw it: (1) in the year you contributed the excess amount; (2) in the following year; (3) in the year you were sent a Notice of Assessment for the year you made the overcontribution; or (4) in the year following that. It would appear that the penalty tax applies until you withdraw the excess overcontribution. These rules may seem confusing, given that Revenue Canada also says that the penalty tax must be paid no later than 90 days after the end of the year in which the excess contribution exists. But Revenue Canada may waive the penalty if you can demonstrate that the overcontribution was inadvertent and that you are taking reasonable steps to eliminate it. If you're in this situation, you may want to take a look at Revenue Canada's tax guide *RRSP and Other Registered Plans for Retirement*. If all else fails, you can also get help by contacting your local taxation office, which should be able to clarify your situation.

Choosing an RRSP

You can get an RRSP at any major financial institutions—banks, trust companies, credit unions, and brokers. Financial advisers may be able to set up your RRSP too. You can also buy an RRSP directly from a mutual fund. You can even request that Canada Savings Bonds, purchased through a financial institution, be designated as an RRSP. Registered Retirement Savings Plans come in all shapes and sizes. Choosing the right one for you requires a bit of careful thought. Going into the bank and asking for an RRSP is not going to cut it.

You'll be offered a huge choice. Do you want a plan based on savings deposits or Guaranteed Investment Certificates (GICs)? Both are extremely safe, but the rate of return may be pretty low. Do you want one of the bank's family of mutual funds and if so, which one? You can have an equity fund (one that invests in the stock market), a bond fund, or a balanced fund, which has a balance of different types of investments, probably including stocks, bonds, and cash. There are funds that invest in overseas stocks and funds that invest in money markets (that is, government Treasury Bills or similar safe investments). All involve different degrees of risk and offer widely varying rates of return.

To be eligible as an RRSP, these investments must meet certain criteria. For example, a mutual fund that invests in different markets may not hold more than 20 percent of its portfolio in foreign investments. Effectively, financial institutions put together packages of investments that meet the criteria and offer them to customers as RRSPs. You can also invest directly in funds offered by mutual fund companies, as long as they meet the criteria for RRSPs. Almost all mutual fund companies have a variety of funds that are eligible for RRSPs. You can buy these directly from the fund company or through your broker. In effect, these are all "off-the-shelf" RRSPs because they are designed and packaged as a stand-alone retirement savings plan that can be purchased directly by an investor.

Like any investment, choosing the right RRSP for you is very much a personal matter. Your choice will depend on the kind of answers you give to a few basic questions. How comfortable are you with taking investment risks? What kind of return would you like to have on your investment? Are you willing to take moderate risks in anticipation of getting a better rate of return? If so, you may want to have at least some of your RRSP funds invested in good-quality stocks. Or are you only comfortable with super-safe investments that will offer a lower rate of return? If so, that probably means buying

GICs (Guaranteed Investment Certificates). How long do you have to go until retirement? The longer the time you have, the longer the time you have available to recover from investment mistakes, such as a drop in the stock market. If your risk tolerance is somewhere in between, you may be more comfortable with a balanced fund, which will offer you a better rate of return than GICs and less investment risk than a portfolio limited to stocks.

Low Risk, Low Return

In the days of high interest rates, many people chose GICs for their RRSPs. These investments are easy to buy. Every bank, trust company, or credit union has them. And there's really no difference —except perhaps slight variations in the interest rates—between a GIC issued by one particular financial institution and a GIC from another. Deposit insurance, backed by the government, covers investments with most banks, trust companies, and credit unions as long as the investment plus interest is not more than $60,000 (limits may be somewhat higher in the case of credit unions) and as long as the investment is made for a period of not more than five years. Within these limits, you are protected in the unlikely event that the financial institution that issued your GIC goes under. What's more, you are guaranteed to get the rate of return promised and there is no investment risk. For nervous investors, GICs are ideal.

But as interest rates have dropped, GICs are losing their appeal. More and more investors have switched to mutual funds. In the fall of 1996, a five-year GIC paid an annual compound rate of interest of only about 4.5 percent. A two-year GIC paid about 3.25 percent a year in compound interest. In comparison, the average annual compound rate of return for Canadian balanced funds over the five-year period to the end of October 1996 was 10.6 percent.

Over a longer period of time, such a wide difference in the rate of return can make a huge difference to the amount you can accumulate in your RRSP. For example, suppose you invested $5,000 in a GIC paying an average annual compound rate of return of 5 percent over a 10-year period. At the end of 10 years, your $5,000 would have increased to about $8,140. But if you had invested $5,000 in an investment paying an average annual compound rate of return of 10.5 percent, at the end of 10 years, you would have $13,570.

As people have shifted away from GICs because of very low rates of return, some financial institutions have tried to improve the rates of return on their GICs by linking the rate paid to the performance of the stock market. This compromise solution may suit you if you really want to stick with a no-risk investment but are reluctant to accept the low rates of return that more traditional GICs are paying. New financial products are coming onto the market all the time. You may want to check with the banks, trust companies, or credit unions to see what kind of new low-risk off-the-shelf RRSPs they may now be offering.

Canada Savings Bonds (CSBs) are another option if you're looking for an absolutely safe investment for your RRSP. While it has always been possible to invest in CSBs if you had a self-directed RRSP, the government has now made them available as an off-the-shelf RRSP. You may buy the bonds through your regular financial institution or broker and request that they be registered as your RRSP. But in an environment of low interest rates, CSBs suffer the same general problems as GICs. While these bonds are absolutely safe, since they are issued by the federal government, the rate of return you will receive will be relatively low compared with other types of investments, such as mutual funds or investing in the stock market where, in exchange for taking more of an investment risk, you can potentially earn a much higher rate of return. Over the longer term, holding most of your RRSP funds in investments that offer a low rate of return will make it very difficult to build up a decent retirement fund for yourself.

Mutual Funds

If you're thinking of investing in a mutual fund, you can check the rates of return of the various funds you're considering in the mutual fund tables published in the financial newspapers. You'll find the funds arranged into groups according to the type of fund—equities, bonds, money market funds, and so on—and the tables indicate which of the funds are eligible for RRSPs. Look for funds with consistently good rates of return over long periods of time. For instance, check the average annual rate of return of the fund over the last three, five, and ten years. But remember, too, that fund managers may change, and rates of return achieved in the past are not necessarily guaranteed in the future. Here again, you need to do your homework. Massive amounts of information are published about various funds and groups of funds. You'll need to sort through the information and decide what appeals to you and what meets your particular needs.

There are no hard and fast rules about this. The best way to decide, again, is to do your homework, read up on investing, and try to get as much information as you can. Above all, try to determine what kind of investor you are and how comfortable you are with investment risk. Remember, too, if you choose a quality mutual fund, you are buying the services of a professional fund manager. As discussed before, these investments should be considered a long-term proposition. Once you've made your decision, resist the temptation to switch back and forth between funds with market ups and downs.

Conventional Wisdom

According to conventional wisdom, as you get closer to retirement, you should move your RRSP funds into safer types of investments, even if these offer a somewhat lower rate of return. The reasoning behind this, of course, is that if you have your RRSP invested in the stock market, you wouldn't want to be in the position of having your plan mature or needing to take out cash at a point when the stock market is down. Thinking ahead should prevent this from happening. If the market is up and you're getting close to retirement, that may be the point to switch your equity funds into GICs.

Another bit of conventional wisdom says that you shouldn't hold stocks in your RRSP at all. That's because the favourable tax treatment given to dividends on Canadian stocks and to capital gains made when you sell investments is not available if you hold these investments in an RRSP. Some advisers say you should keep your stock investments outside your RRSP and use your RRSP to hold interest-bearing investments like GICs. That advice is fine for people who have lots of money to invest. But, if you're like most women, your RRSP is probably the only kind of investment portfolio you have. And financial advisers also warn that unless you hold at least some stocks in your RRSP, you'll have no real protection against inflation. That's because, in the long term, prices on the stock market tend to rise, providing a form of inflation indexing for investors.

There are always exceptions to these rules and you will have to decide for yourself where you want to go with your RRSP. The most important thing is to get as much information as you can and to consider your decision carefully. It's your financial security in retirement that's at stake here. The good news is that there is no shortage of advice. All financial institutions have free booklets and other information about the RRSPs they offer. Financial planners can advise you—although you should be aware that some of them earn commissions from selling mutual funds, so be cautious of free advice. In the end, there's no getting away from the fact that you have to make up your own mind.

Self-Directed Plans

An alternative to buying an RRSP "off the shelf" is setting up a self-directed plan, where you get to choose the mix of investments. You can then include such exotic items as strip coupons and even the mortgage on your own house—although most experts don't recommend the latter. You can select a mix of mutual funds and direct investments in the stock market, or any combination of investments that you like. However, you may not have more than 20 percent of your self-directed RRSP in foreign investments, but that's based on the "book value" or purchase price and not on the current market value of your plan. If you already hold stocks, bonds, or other investments that are eligible for your RRSP, you may transfer them to your RRSP, as long as the current fair market value of the investments transferred is within your regular RRSP contribution limit. In other words, you can make an RRSP contribution "in kind."

Some of the experts say that once the funds in your off-the-shelf RRSPs get to about $50,000, you should be thinking about combining them all in a self-directed plan. Others put the minimum limit for a self-directed plan much higher.

A self-directed plan can be set up by all the same financial institutions or brokers who offer off-the-shelf RRSPs. But the self-directed plan must have a trustee, which the financial institution or broker will also arrange. The trustee is responsible for keeping the records, making sure you invest only in eligible investments, and so on. You'll generally pay an administrative fee of anywhere from about $100 to $300 a year to the financial institution that runs your self-directed RRSP. Some brokers and other financial institutions may even have a no-fee self-directed RRSP, but the choice of investments for these plans may be limited.

Having a self-directed plan may be a good idea if you're an experienced investor, because you can then play an active role in managing your investments to accumulate a good fund for your retirement. It may also be more convenient, if you have a number of off-the-shelf RRSPs in various places, to combine them all in one self-directed plan so you get only one annual statement and everything is neat and tidy. But there's probably not much point in setting up a self-directed plan if you don't need that kind of convenience and you're not interested in selecting and managing a portfolio of investments for your retirement.

Spousal Plans

There's one feature of the RRSP system that's particularly helpful to women who may not have much income of their own on which to base an RRSP contribution. A person may contribute to an RRSP for his or her spouse. Suppose your husband or partner wants to set up an RRSP for you; he may use part of his own contribution limit to contribute to a plan in your name, known as a "spousal" RRSP. There is no extra contribution limit for people to contribute to spousal plans; these contributions must be made within the contributor's own RRSP limit. And if your husband or partner is contributing for you, he gets to claim the tax deduction.

The plan is yours, though. However, be aware that if you take money out of a spousal plan and he contributed to any spousal plan for you in any of the past three years (even if it was a different plan from the one you're taking the money from), the amount you withdraw is attributed to him. That is, he has to declare it and pay tax on it. Common-law spouses may set up spousal plans for each other, but such plans are not available to same-sex couples because the Income Tax Act doesn't recognize such relationships.

Generally speaking, funds in your RRSP may not be transferred to your spouse's RRSP or vice versa. But exceptions are allowed: (1) where one spouse dies; (2) where the transfer is made under a decree, order, or judgment of a court; (3) where the transfer is made under a written separation agreement; or (4) where the purpose of transferring funds is to settle rights arising out of your marriage on or after the breakdown of the marriage.

Contributing to a spousal RRSP can be a way of income-splitting between spouses, and it is especially advantageous if one spouse does not work outside the home. Effectively, it's a way of transferring some of a couple's retirement income to the lower-income spouse, thereby lowering the taxes that the couple will have to pay on their joint retirement income. For instance, when you and your spouse get to retirement age, the person with the lower income will have some of the RRSP funds to withdraw, and these funds will be taxed at a lower rate than if they'd been left in the hands of the spouse with the higher income. But not only is this strategy a way of lowering the couple's tax burden in retirement, it also gives a woman who has not worked outside the home some retirement income in her own name and under her own control.

Taking Money Out of Your RRSP

There's nothing to prevent you from taking money out of your RRSP at any time, but if you do, you will have to add the withdrawal to your income and pay tax on it when you file your tax return. If you make a lump-sum withdrawal from your plan, the financial institution is required to withhold part of the tax due. The amount withheld depends on how much you withdraw. For amounts up to and including $5,000, the withholding tax is 10 percent. On amounts over $5,000, up to and including $15,000, 20 percent of the entire amount withdrawn will be withheld. And if you take out more than $15,000, 30 percent will be withheld from the entire amount withdrawn. Withholding rates are different in Quebec. If you live in that province, the rate is: 21 percent on the first $5,000; 30 percent on amounts over $5,000 and up to and including $15,000; and 35 percent on amounts over $15,000.

The amounts withheld are really a pre-payment of part of the extra tax you may owe when you declare the withdrawal at tax time.

Depending on your other income, you may have to pay additional tax at that time. Or, some of the tax withheld may be refunded to you.

Using Your RRSP for Other Purposes

As noted earlier, you are free to use your RRSP for purposes other than retirement. For example, many women use RRSP funds to finance a maternity leave. But be warned. If you take money out of your plan for this or any other purpose, you'll lose the benefit of interest compounding on the funds you withdraw. Even if you can make up for the withdrawal by using part of your contribution limit to contribute an equivalent amount, you will have lost the benefit of tax-free compounding of interest on the funds you withdrew. And you may never be able to make up for that loss of interest. If there's one word of advice more crucial than any other about using your RRSP for other purposes, it's "don't."

The Home Buyers' Plan

Unfortunately, the government itself is not blameless on this issue. A few years, ago, it introduced the Home Buyers' Plan, which allows first-time home buyers to tap into their RRSP savings for the down payment on a home. To the extent that a home is another way of providing for your financial security in old age (a topic discussed later in Chapter 8), perhaps the government thought there was nothing wrong with encouraging Canadians to use their retirement savings in this way. But if you take advantage of this plan, you may end up with less money in your retirement nest egg when you want to retire.

The Home Buyers' Plan lets you borrow up to $20,000 from your RRSP to put toward the purchase of a home without paying tax on the money you withdraw. If you're married, whether in a formal marriage or a common-law relationship, both you and your spouse or partner may each withdraw $20,000 from your RRSP (therefore, $40,000 altogether) under the program. In fact, even a same-sex couple or several friends may each withdraw up to $20,000 from their RRSPs to put toward the joint purchase of a home, as long as they qualify for the program. The program may be used only by a first-time buyer, that is, as defined by the program, someone who has not owned and lived in a home as a principal residence during the five calendar years up to and including the current year. If your spouse owned and lived in a home during that period and you lived in the home as your principal place of residence, you would not qualify for the program.

The program has strict rules. Withdrawals have to be noted on a special form that states you have signed an agreement to purchase a home and indicating where it is located. Once it has this form, the financial institution holding your RRSP will allow you to take the necessary funds out of your RRSP without withholding any tax. Once you have taken the funds out of your RRSP, you must actually acquire the home before October 1 of the year following the year in which you withdrew the funds. As well, you must use the home as your principal residence not later than one year after you buy it.

There are also rules about paying back the money you have "borrowed" from yourself. In the second year following the year in which you took out the money, you must start repaying it. You may spread your repayments over a 15-year period in 15 equal annual instalments. You are not required to pay interest to yourself on this loan. If you fail to make the required payment each year, the amount of the missed payment will have to be included in your income for that year and will then be taxable. If you repay less than the required amount, the shortfall would also have to be included in your income for that year.

Taking money out of your RRSP under the Home Buyers' Plan may affect the amount you are allowed to contribute to your RRSP in the year you make the withdrawal. If you participate in the Home Buyers' Plan, you may not be able to deduct for any year all or part of the contributions you make to your RRSP during the 89-day period immediately before you withdraw an amount under the Home Buyers' Plan. Revenue Canada's guide *RRSP and Other Registered Plans for Retirement* explains how to calculate this.

Think carefully before you decide to use some of your retirement savings to purchase a home and take a look at the section called "Turning a Home into a Pension" in Chapter 8. If you still want to go ahead with the idea, you may want to check with your local taxation office (listed in your telephone book under Revenue Canada Taxation) for more information about this program.

When Your RRSP Matures

The rules say you must convert your RRSP to some form of income by the end of the year in which you reach the age of 69. The age used to be 71, but the 1996 federal budget announced that it would be lowered to 69, starting with the 1997 tax year. Once your RRSP matures, you have several choices. You can take out all the money in a lump sum, of course, but that's not a good idea. For one thing, you would have to include the entire amount in your income for that year and pay tax on it at your top tax rate. Besides, if you've managed to hang on to your RRSP until you're 69, your best option is to turn it into a regular pension for yourself.

There are a couple of ways to do this. One is to purchase an annuity, which was described earlier in Chapter 5. The other, and by far the most popular, option is to turn your plan into a Registered Retirement Income Fund (RRIF).

Registered Retirement Income Funds

Essentially, a RRIF works just like an RRSP, with one important difference. Instead of putting money into the plan, you are taking it out. Each year, you must withdraw a certain minimum amount, which is calculated as a percentage of the fair market value of your plan at the beginning of the year and is based on your age. The idea is to withdraw amounts in such a way that the RRIF continues to provide you with an income for the rest of your life.

The government establishes the percentage amount that must be withdrawn and the percentage increases gradually each year as you get older, starting at just over 7 percent at age 71 and rising to 20 percent by the time you reach the age of 94 (assuming that you reach that age). For married couples, the RRIF withdrawals can be based on the age of the younger spouse so that the funds last longer. Originally, the rules for RRIF withdrawals were based on the assumption that the RRIF funds would be used up by the age of 90. Those rules were changed a few years ago, and withdrawals may now, in effect, continue for the rest of your life.

The table below shows the percentage of the assets in your RRIF that must be withdrawn each year, as set out in income tax regulations. Although the government has now reduced the age at which a RRIF must begin from age 71 to age 69, apparently it does not intend to publish a new minimum withdrawal table. While the table starts at 71, you may convert your RRSP to a RRIF at any age. Generally speaking, it's better to postpone converting your RRSP to a RRIF as long as you can, so that your retirement fund can go on earning a return for you as long as possible before you start to withdraw the funds. If you decide to convert your funds to a RRIF at an earlier age, the minimum withdrawal is the opening balance in the RRIF at the beginning of the year divided by the number you get when you subtract your age at the beginning of that year from 90. For example, if you were 55 years old and had $50,000 in your RRIF at the beginning of the year, your minimum withdrawal that year would be $50,000 divided by 35 (90 – 55), or $1429, which is 2.86 percent of the amount in your plan. You are not required to start making withdrawals from your RRIF until the year after the year in which you establish the plan.

Minimum Annual RRIF Withdrawals

Age	Minimum Withdrawal %	Age	Minimum Withdrawal %
71	7.38	84	9.93
72	7.48	85	10.33
73	7.59	86	10.79
74	7.71	87	11.33
75	7.85	88	11.96
76	7.99	89	12.71
77	8.15	90	13.62
78	8.33	91	14.73
79	8.53	92	16.12
80	8.75	93	17.92
81	8.99	94	20.00
82	9.27	95	20.00
83	9.58	96	20.00

The financial institution holding your plan will determine the fair market value on which the minimum withdrawal has to be based. In fact, the financial institution will also tell you what minimum amount must be withdrawn, which depends on your age. The amounts you withdraw each year have to be declared when you file your tax return and will be subject to income tax. Of course, you can arrange to have the withdrawals paid to you in a lump sum or in the form of a regular monthly income.

In the meantime, as you are making the withdrawals, the rest of your RRIF remains invested and continues to earn a return. In fact, if the value of the investments in your plan increases by more than the amount withdrawn each year, your plan will go on providing you with retirement income that should keep pace with inflation, until you reach a ripe old age.

When you're thinking about investments for your RRIF, you can follow the same strategy as you would for an RRSP, as described earlier. The choice depends on your own personal objectives, degree of comfort with investment risk, and so on. But you'll want to keep in mind that, if you need your RRIF income to live on, you'll have to have investments that can be easily turned into cash so you can make the minimum withdrawals. For example, if your RRIF is invested in GICs that don't mature until four years from now, you will have a problem cashing them in before the maturity date to provide the funds you need to make your minimum RRIF withdrawal. The financial institution holding your plan may ask you to pay an interest rate penalty to compensate for the fact that your funds were not invested with them for as long as you had agreed. Like an RRSP, you can buy a RRIF "off-the-shelf" from the same financial institutions that sell RRSPs, or you can set up a self-directed RRIF. And the same considerations apply as those discussed in connection with RRSPs in choosing one or the other. In fact, if you already have an RRSP with a particular financial institution, you can generally get them to roll over the investments into a RRIF without making any other changes. In effect, your RRSP just becomes a RRIF and you start taking the money out.

While the minimum withdrawal from your RRIF is specified, you may take out more than the minimum if you wish. However, if you take out more, the amount in excess of the minimum will be treated as a lump-sum withdrawal, and the financial institution will have to withhold tax, in the same way as it would if you made a lump-sum withdrawal from an RRSP. Of course, if you want your RRIF to provide you with a pension for the rest of your life, you'll have to resist the temptation to withdraw extra amounts.

Do's and Don'ts of RRSPs

To sum it all up, here's a list of do's and don'ts for your private retirement savings:

- Put as much as you can into your RRSP each year.
- If you're contributing a lump sum, try to contribute early in the year so that your money can earn a return for as long as possible.
- Set up a monthly payment plan with your bank, trust company, credit union, or mutual fund, so you don't have to come up with a big lump sum each year to make your contribution.
- Resolve to do your homework and to take your time selecting the right kind of RRSP for you.
- Plan ahead. Don't rush down to your financial institution at the last minute to get your RRSP just before the deadline.
- Choose your RRSP investments carefully and make sure you're comfortable with the type of investments you have chosen.
- Get your spouse to contribute to a plan in your name if you don't have your own earned income to make your own contribution.
- Don't be tempted to cash in your plan to finance your maternity leave or to use the funds for anything other than retirement.

CHAPTER 7

HOW MARRIAGE OR A RELATIONSHIP CAN AFFECT YOUR PENSION

If you have a spouse or partner, you're likely to face a much more secure financial future than someone who has never been married. But, being married may be detrimental to your retirement income in some circumstances, especially now that the federal government is proposing to get rid of Old Age Security in 2001 and replace it with a new Seniors Benefit, which will be income-tested and based on family income. On a more positive note, though, sooner or later pension benefits from your spouse's workplace pension or CPP may supplement your own retirement savings to boost your pension income. It can happen in a variety of ways. You could share his CPP pension when you both reach retirement age. If he dies, you may receive a surviving spouse pension, both from his CPP and his workplace pension plan. If you get divorced, you will likely be entitled to a share in the pension he has accumulated during your marriage, both through the CPP and through his workplace pension. He can even make a contribution to your retirement savings by putting money into an RRSP for you. On the other side of the ledger is the fact that when the new Seniors Benefit is introduced in 2001, your eligibility for a benefit in your own name will probably depend on his income.

Almost all these provisions apply to common-law spouses as well as to those in a traditional marriage. Generally speaking, they don't apply to same-sex couples, although more and more workplace pension plans are making provisions for the surviving spouse of a same-sex couple to receive a surviving spouse pension when the spouse who belonged to the pension plan dies.

It goes without saying that if you are in a relationship, you should make it your business to find out how your spouse or partner's pension plan will contribute to your retirement savings in a variety of circumstances, including staying together, and being left alone through divorce, death, or the breakdown of your relationship.

You'd think by now that everyone would have accepted the concept of retirement planning for couples as something that should involve both spouses, but I'm still astounded by how many women are in the dark about the retirement plans of their spouses. That's why talking with Brenda was such an eye-opener. This 49-year-old full-time homemaker from Prince Edward Island told me, "I leave the planning up to my husband. I let someone else do all the paperwork." Although Brenda was in the paid work force for a brief period before her children were born, she didn't belong to a pension plan and didn't even know if there was one. She thinks her husband may have a workplace pension plan, but she doesn't know for sure. And although he contributes to an RRSP for her, she has no idea how much money is in her plan. Brenda lets her husband handle all the finances. She has no money of her own and she will be completely dependent on her husband to support her in her old age. Maybe Brenda needs to wake up and smell the coffee! At the very least, she should find out what provisions have been made for her retirement, whether she finds them acceptable, and how they might be affected if her husband is no longer on the scene.

Sharing a Pension at Retirement

Sharing your spouse or partner's pension income when you both retire may be something you've just assumed you'd do—just as you pool your joint income, or depend on your partner for financial support, before retirement. But that's an informal arrangement. It may even be possible to apply for a formal sharing of some pension income so that you each get a cheque in your own name when you retire.

Basic Benefits from Government Programs

As explained in Chapter 4, some government programs are based on family income. You should note that, while these programs are said to depend on "family income," effectively they are based on the joint income of both spouses. If you're a widow living with one of your adult children and his or her family, for instance, the income of these other family members is not taken into account to determine whether or not you're eligible for a benefit. If you're in this situation, you would, in effect, be treated as a single individual. But if you're married, whether you're in a formal marriage or a common-law relationship, your eligibility for the Guaranteed Income Supplement or Spouse's Allowance will depend on your spouse or partner's and your joint income. Once your eligibility is established, however, you will receive a cheque in your own name. This is also the way the new Seniors Benefit will work when it is introduced in 2001, although the current Old Age Security benefit is paid to individuals and effectively is income-tested based on individual income.

This first tier of the retirement income system, where programs are mainly focused on preventing poverty among seniors, is the one area where being married—whether it's a formal marriage or a common-law relationship—can mean lower benefits for you as an individual, than if you were unattached or single. Where benefits are based on family income, each spouse gets a lower individual benefit than a single person would. However, some provincial programs, which top up benefits for low-income seniors, give higher benefits to each spouse of a married couple than they would to single individuals.

Generally, though, the theory is that two people living together can save on expenses, so each spouse needs less individually than she or he would require if they were living on their own.

The same reasoning is not applied to spouses in a same-sex relationship. In fact, in a landmark case, decided by a majority of the Supreme Court of Canada in May 1995 (*Egan v. Canada*, [1995] 2 Supreme Court Record 513), John Nesbit was denied a Spouse's Allowance benefit because his relationship with James Egan did not fall within the definition of "spouse" in the Old Age Security Act, although the Court said the two men had lived together since 1948 "in a relationship marked by commitment and interdependence similar to that which one expects to find in a marriage." Dissenting justices on the Court said that, while the Old Age Security Act defines spouses as being "persons of the opposite sex," the definition should be broadened to include people in a relationship analogous to marriage.

While same-sex relationships may eventually be officially recognized for pension purposes, under the existing rules, same-sex spouses may each receive benefits from this first tier of the retirement income system as if they were two separate individuals. In other words, same-sex couples generally receive higher benefits from the first tier of the retirement income system than opposite-sex couples. Mr. Nesbit applied for a Spouse's Allowance. As discussed in Chapter 4, you can only get the Spouse's Allowance if you are married to a low-income pensioner or if you are a low-income widow who has not remarried. Unfortunately for John Nesbit, he wasn't entitled to this benefit because he didn't fit these criteria. He couldn't get benefits as a "spouse" because he didn't fit the definition of "spouse," nor could he get benefits as a single individual since he had never been married. The Spouse's Allowance program discriminates against claimants on the basis of marital status: it doesn't give benefits to low-income people who have never been married.

Sharing a CPP Retirement Pension

As explained earlier, you are entitled to share your spouse's CPP retirement pension, whether or not you yourself have contributed to the plan. The provision is known as "assignment" and was discussed in detail in Chapter 4. Assignment is a voluntary arrangement, although some women's groups have suggested it should be mandatory. Either you or your spouse can apply to share your combined pensions, but the sharing arrangements can't be backdated. If you have a much lower CPP pension than your spouse or partner, or if you are not entitled to a CPP retirement pension of your own, sharing his CPP pension would give you a benefit in your own name and is a way of equalizing the benefits you each get from the CPP. It's also a way of saving on taxes, as mentioned earlier. If more of the higher-income spouse's CPP pension can be received by the lower-income spouse, the couple together may pay less tax. But if you're already entitled to a CPP pension in your own name and it's not that much different from your spouse's, assignment won't hold any advantages for you.

For CPP purposes, a "spouse" is a person of the opposite sex with whom you are in a legal or common-law marriage. If you want to share a CPP pension with a common-law spouse, you must have been living in a conjugal relationship for at least one year. You can get an application form for pension assignment from your local Income Security Programs office.

If you set up a pension-sharing arrangement, the arrangement will end: if you and your spouse ask the CPP to end it; in the twelfth month after you separate; in the month you divorce; if one of you has never paid into the CPP (or into the Quebec Pension Plan) and begins contributing; or the month one of you dies.

Sharing a Workplace Pension

Men are more likely than women to be members of a workplace pension plan, although the gap is narrowing quickly. At last count (in

1993), about 51 percent of men, compared with 44 percent of women, who had paid work belonged to a workplace pension plan. Your chances of being married to someone with a workplace pension may be only 50-50, but if your spouse or partner does have a plan at work, you will be entitled to various benefits.

The amount of your spouse's retirement pension will depend on issues such as the type of plan he has and the terms and conditions of the benefit (see Chapter 5). Chances are his pension will be based on his own earnings and length of service—a defined benefit pension —although it could be a defined contribution plan, which won't guarantee any specific pension. He won't get an additional retirement benefit for having a spouse or common-law partner. In fact, if he wants his workplace pension plan to provide a benefit to his surviving spouse, his retirement pension may be less than it would be if he had no spouse, as explained later. But his pension should be factored in to your replacement income needs as a couple, as was explained in Chapter 3. If you both belong to a workplace pension plan, his pension will probably be higher than yours, since most men who belong to workplace pension plans have higher earnings and longer service than female pension plan members.

Be careful not to overestimate the amount of his pension. He may not stay with the same employer until he retires, and may therefore end up with amounts in a locked-in retirement account (LIRA) instead of a benefit related to his earnings or years of service. Check to see if he has an indexed pension. As explained earlier, most workplace pensions are not automatically indexed for inflation. Even at low rates of inflation, the purchasing power of a fixed benefit can quickly be eroded. For example, a pensioner who begins retirement at the age of 65 with a pension of $800 a month will find his benefit is worth only $506 after 15 years, assuming inflation averages 3 percent a year.

The same kinds of considerations apply if you're trying to assess the retirement income of a same-sex partner and how that might contribute to your replacement income goals as a couple while you are both living together.

Marriage and RRSPs

If you have little or no earned income of your own, your spouse may use part of his RRSP contribution limit to contribute to an RRSP in your name—generally referred to as a "spousal" RRSP. Until fairly recently, this provision could be used only by legally married spouses. But since January 1, 1993, it has also been available to common-law couples. For income tax purposes, a common-law spouse is defined as a person of the opposite sex with whom you have a conjugal relationship. You must have cohabited for at least 12 months. Even if you haven't lived together for a year, you may still qualify if you and your partner are the parents of a child. The child could be natural or adopted, or one for whom one of the partners has assumed financial support, even if not formally adopted. If you want to make use of the RRSP provisions available to common-law spouses, but you're not sure if you fit the definition, you may want to check with your local tax office for more details.

Like the Canada Pension Plan, the Income Tax Act does not recognize same-sex spouses, so they are not able to contribute to spousal RRSPs.

The rationale behind a spousal RRSP is that the spouse with the higher income—generally the husband—can contribute to an RRSP for the spouse with the lower income—generally the wife—so that when both reach retirement, the income generated by their RRSPs (at that point converted to RRIFs or annuities) will be more evenly distributed between the spouses, thus reducing their tax burden. But some couples overlook the fact that contributing to a spousal RRSP only makes sense from a tax point of view if the spouse who benefits from the spousal plan will also have the lower income when they both retire. Of course there may be other altruistic reasons why a higher-earning spouse might want to share some of his or her earnings with a lower-earning spouse by contributing to a spousal RRSP in her or his name. But assuming they are still together when they retire, they will save on taxes only if contributing to the spousal RRSP earlier will result in the RRSP funds being in the hands of the spouse who has the lower income at retirement.

For instance, let's suppose Fred and Susan are both in the paid work force, and Fred earns quite a bit more than Susan. They decide that Fred will use part of his RRSP contribution limit to contribute to a spousal plan for Susan. But Susan, who works for a big corporation, subsequently rises rapidly up the corporate ladder. Her earnings increase faster than Fred's do. And what's more, she has a good workplace pension and Fred doesn't have one at all. Even though Fred earns more than Susan right now, it makes no sense for him to contribute to a spousal RRSP for her, because when they both retire, she will likely have a better pension than he will. When they're added to her pension income, the funds from her spousal RRSP will be taxed at a higher rate than they would have been if Fred had put them into his own RRSP instead. The moral of this story is, think carefully before deciding whether a spousal RRSP is a good idea, and, if so, which spouse should contribute to it.

Contributing to a Spousal RRSP

No additional RRSP contribution room is given to spouses who want to contribute to an RRSP in the other spouse's name. The spouse making the contribution may use part of his own limit to contribute to a plan in the other spouse's name, but he doesn't get an extra contribution allowance. And the spouse making the contribution claims the deduction at tax time. For instance, suppose your spouse has an RRSP contribution limit of $10,000 this year. He decides to contribute $4,000 to his own RRSP and $6,000 to a spousal plan for you.

When he files his income tax return, he will be entitled to deduct the entire $10,000 from his income for tax purposes. But because the spousal RRSP is in your name, it belongs to you.

As noted earlier, an RRSP must be converted to a stream of income by the end of the year in which the holder reaches the age of 69 (previously 71). But if your husband or partner is contributing to an RRSP in your name, he can go on making the contributions until the end of the year in which you reach age 69, even if he is then much older. However, you should note that he can only do that if he continues to have earned income that entitles him to make an RRSP contribution.

Setting Up a Spousal Plan

All the same financial institutions, brokers, and mutual fund companies that set up RRSPs can set up a spousal RRSP for you. But it will generally have to be kept separate from an RRSP to which you make your own contributions. Although technically, there's no reason why you and your spouse can't contribute to the same plan as long as it's in your name only, most financial institutions will not permit it because of the difficulty of keeping track of who made which contributions. At the end of each year, the financial institution has to supply a tax information slip to the contributor so he or she can deduct the contribution for tax purposes. If both spouses are contributing to the same plan, that becomes a serious administrative problem. However, some full-service brokers apparently have set up their computer systems to keep track of spousal contributions and regular contributions made to one spouse's RRSP by both individuals. If this is something you're interested in doing, you may want to check with your broker or financial institution to see what that company's policy is. But you should be aware that if you set up such an arrangement, the plan becomes a spousal plan and will be subject to restrictions on withdrawals as described in the next section.

Another thing to keep in mind is that the rules do not allow spouses to have joint RRSPs, so there's no way you can have one plan in both your names.

Withdrawing Funds from a Spousal RRSP

Although contributions to your spousal plan have been made by your spouse, only you can withdraw funds from the plan. Generally speaking, any amounts you take out of your plan will have to be included in your income in the year you withdraw the funds, just as they would with a regular RRSP. But with a spousal plan, there are some special provisions. If you take money out of your spousal plan and your spouse has contributed to that plan—or to any other spousal plan in your name—in the year you withdraw the funds or in either of the two preceding years, the amounts you withdraw will have to be included in his income and he will have to pay the tax on them. It's important to note that even if your spouse hasn't made any recent contributions to the spousal plan from which you're making the withdrawal, he may still have to declare your withdrawal from that plan as part of his income if he has contributed to any other spousal RRSP in the year you make the withdrawal or in the two preceding years.

For instance, suppose it's September and you have $10,000 sitting in a spousal RRSP that you've had for five years, and that amount is invested in Guaranteed Investment Certificates (GICs) that have just matured. Your husband also decided a few years ago to start a second spousal plan, invested in a mutual fund, and has been contributing $3,000 a year to that plan every July for the past four years. You decide to cash in the GIC plan this year and use the money to finance your maternity leave. He will have to include part of your withdrawal in his income this year, even though he has made no contributions to that plan for the past five years, because he did contribute to some other spousal plan in the year you took the money out of your GIC plan. The amount he will have to declare is the lesser of the amount you withdrew ($10,000) and the total amounts he contributed to all spousal plans for you in the year of withdrawal and the two preceding years ($9,000). In this example, then, he would have to include $9,000 in his income in the year you make the withdrawal.

Exceptions to this rule are allowed if you have separated and are living apart because of marriage breakdown at the time you make the withdrawals from your spousal plan, and in some other circumstances. If your spousal RRSP has been converted to a RRIF within the three-year period and you start receiving regular payments (as you are required to do once the RRIF is established), they will count as your income, even if your spouse contributed to a spousal RRSP in the year you start RRIF withdrawals or in either of the two preceding years. But this only applies if your RRIF withdrawal does not exceed the minimum withdrawal amount (see Chapter 6). If you take out more than the minimum within the three-year limitation period, the excess would be attributed to your spouse and he would have to pay tax on it.

Sharing a Pension If Your Relationship Ends

If your relationship ends, you may be entitled to a share of the pension accumulated by your spouse or partner during the marriage. Division of pension credits on divorce or separation is provided for in the Canada Pension Plan and you may also be entitled to a share in your spouse's workplace pension, if he has one. In this way, even if you don't belong to a pension plan at work or contribute to the CPP yourself, you could end up with a pension of your own at retirement, or you may find yourself with a lump sum as part of a divorce settlement, which you can invest to provide a retirement income for yourself. Getting a share of the pension benefit accumulated by your spouse or partner if your relationship ends can also add to the retirement income you've been able to accumulate on your own. No one wants her marriage to end in divorce or her relationship to break down, so planning ahead for this kind of eventuality may not be easy. But forewarned is forearmed, as they say, and it's better to know what may happen to your pension or retirement income if the unthinkable happens.

Credit-Splitting in the CPP

You'll be glad to know that the Canada Pension Plan recognizes that in a legal marriage or common-law relationship, regardless of whether or not both spouses work outside the home, both share in the building of their assets and entitlements, including pension entitlements being built up in the CPP. That's why the CPP provides for pension entitlements built up during the marriage or common-law relationship to be divided equally between the spouses if the relationship ends. (The QPP divides only those credits earned during marriage.) The process is usually referred to as "credit-splitting." As noted earlier (see Chapter 4), many women who went through a divorce or separation in the past missed out on this opportunity because they didn't know it existed. As well, many women gave up their right to a share of their spouse's CPP credits on marriage breakdown, in exchange for some other consideration.

It's important to remember that, once the credits are divided between you and your spouse they become part of your record of earnings forever. This is not the same as the assignment of a retirement benefit, described earlier. If you set up an assignment arrangement, assuming both partners want it to continue, the part of the benefit "assigned" to you remains yours as long as you live together and are both alive. For example, if your spouse was entitled to a retirement pension in his own right of $500 a month and you were entitled, in your own right, to a retirement pension of $100 a month, an assignment would result in your both receiving $300 a month. If you were then to die before your husband, his retirement pension would revert to $500 a month. If he subsequently remarried and then died, his second wife would be entitled to a survivor benefit based on his $500 a month retirement pension.

While assignment is a redistribution of the retirement pensions, a division of credits on marriage breakdown results in a permanent change to the record of earnings of both former spouses.

What's the advantage of credit-splitting? Generally, it can result in a higher CPP pension for you when you retire. The CPP keeps a record of your "pensionable earnings"—that is, the earnings on which your retirement pension and other CPP benefits will be based. The contributions you pay on these earnings over the years become your "CPP pension credits." As you continue to pay into the plan, your pension credits build up, and when you apply for a benefit, these credits are used to calculate your entitlement. Generally, the more credits you have, the higher your CPP benefit will be.

A credit-splitting arrangement adds up the credits both spouses accumulated in the CPP during the marriage and divides the credits equally between the spouses. Generally, this means that the credits of the lower-income spouse (usually the wife) are increased, while the credits of the higher-income spouse (generally the husband) are decreased by the same amount. The total credits of the couple are not increased, of course. The longer you and your former spouse were together and the bigger the difference between your earnings while you were together, the greater the exchange of credits will be. The arrangement is particularly beneficial if you have not worked outside the home and therefore haven't been able to contribute to the CPP yourself. In this case, credit-splitting will give you a CPP pension in your own name when you retire, based on the share of your spouse's credits allocated to you as a result of your divorce or marriage breakdown. If you decided to go back into the paid work force after your divorce, new credits you earn yourself would be added to those received from your former spouse, to give you a bigger pension when you retire.

But for couples where both were earning and contributing to the CPP, a credit-splitting arrangement is really only beneficial if there is a difference in earnings between the spouses. If your pensionable earnings and your spouse's were the same while you were together, there would be nothing to exchange, so a credit split would not be done.

Couples who are still married or living together in an ongoing relationship are not eligible for credit-splitting, but they may be able to share CPP benefits when both retire. Credit-splitting is not available on the breakdown of a same-sex relationship either.

With a few exceptions, credit-splitting on marriage breakdown is now mandatory for the CPP. Since January 1, 1987, once the CPP has the necessary information about your legal divorce or annulment, your CPP pension credits must be split, unless there is a valid spousal agreement signed in one of the provinces that allow couples to opt out of credit-splitting. The rules on these spousal agreements changed on June 4, 1986. If you signed an agreement before that date, specifically giving up your right to share in a spouse's CPP pension credits, then generally you will not be entitled to a division of CPP credits. However, if it was a general agreement, giving up "all further claims," for example, and it didn't specifically mention CPP pension credits, you may still be able to get some credits from your spouse if you were the lower-income earner.

If you signed an agreement on or after June 4, 1986, even if, according to the agreement, you specifically gave up your right to split CPP credits, in most cases, that statement is not valid and the CPP can still split the pension credits built up during your marriage. But there are exceptions. Provincial laws in Saskatchewan, British Columbia, and Quebec allow couples specifically to agree not to split CPP pension credits. So, if you signed such an agreement in one of those provinces, CPP might not be able to split the credits. At this point, these are the only three provinces that allow opting out of the CPP's mandatory credit-splitting provisions. If you're not sure about your own particular situation, you may want to contact the Income Security Programs office, or if you contributed to the Quebec Pension Plan, contact an office of La Régie des rentes du Québec.

If you have a legal separation or have just ended a common-law relationship, CPP credits can only be split if you or your former spouse choose to apply for it. In these cases, although not in cases of divorce or annulment, the applicant can ask to withdraw the application within 60 days of being notified of the credit split. You might have second thoughts about credit-splitting for some reason; for example, if it turns out you'd get less than you had expected from dividing the credits.

In the case of a divorce that took place after January 1, 1987, you don't have to apply for CPP credit-splitting. All that's necessary is that the CPP authorities be notified that the divorce has occurred. The CPP authorities will also need supporting documentation on how long you lived together. In all other cases—for example, legal separation and common-law relationships—you have to apply for the credit split.

Either you, your former spouse, or your lawyers may request a credit split. And in the case of a legal separation, a signature is required. The information you give the CPP—for example, the length of time you lived together—will affect the credit split, because the amount that is divided depends on credits accumulated during your marriage or common-law relationship. If you're the one applying, the information will be given to your former spouse. And both you and he have the right to challenge the information and to appeal any decision about a division of credits. What if you have remarried or you're living in a new common-law relationship? You can still ask to split credits with your former spouse.

If one of you has contributed to the CPP and the other to the QPP, your credits can still be split, but it's a bit more complicated. If you live in Quebec, you'll need to contact an office of La Régie des rentes du Québec for more information. If you're living in another province or territory, contact an Income Security Programs office (listed in the phone book under Human Resources Development Canada) and that office will be able to explain in detail how this works. Human Resources Development Canada has an excellent free booklet called *Credit-Splitting upon Divorce or Separation*, which explains all this in more detail and gives some examples to show how credit-splitting works. You can get a copy by writing to Public Enquiry Centre, Human Resources Development Canada, Ottawa-Hull K1A 0J9, or faxing a request to (819) 953-7260 and quoting catalogue number ISPB-151-01-95E.

It's important to note that, because credit-splitting is now generally mandatory for couples who divorce, there isn't really a time limit on notifying the Income Security Programs office of your divorce, so you can access your share of your former spouse's CPP credits. But the rules have changed several times in the past 20 years. If your divorce took place some years ago, you may want to check with the Income Security Programs people to see if a credit split is still possible. Remember, if you have a legal separation or have ended a common-law relationship, you must apply for credit-splitting and there are time limits, as explained in Chapter 4. Common-law spouses must apply within four years of starting to live apart. There's no time limit for applying in the case of spouses who have a legal separation, unless your former spouse dies, in which case you must apply within three years of the date of death.

Marriage Breakdown and Workplace Pensions

Next to the family home, a private workplace pension—usually the husband's—is often the biggest asset a couple has at the time of divorce or marriage breakdown. But sharing the benefit is usually not a simple matter. While entitlement to a share in the pension is generally determined according to family law, the way in which that share can be paid out will generally depend on the pension legislation of the relevant jurisdiction. Of course, as noted earlier, you have only a 50 percent chance of being married to a man with a workplace pension plan. But if he does have one and your marriage ends in divorce, you will probably be entitled to a share of the pension in some form or other.

Provincial family law legislation specifies the types of assets that must be shared by the spouses at divorce, but in most provinces these laws apply only to married couples and not to common-law unions. In addition, family laws in various provinces do not always specify that pensions must be included among the assets to be divided, although a decision by the Supreme Court of Canada in 1990 ruled that pension entitlements were part of matrimonial property to be divided between the spouses on marriage breakdown.

Common-law spouses are not always entitled to a share in a workplace pension if their relationship ends, although the provinces of Quebec, Manitoba, Nova Scotia, and Prince Edward Island specifically provide for the division of pensions on the break-up of a common-law union. It may also be possible for a common-law spouse to share in the pension of her former partner in provinces where there are support obligations to a former common-law partner under the family laws of the jurisdiction where they live. If you are faced with the end of a common-law relationship, you may want to check with a lawyer or with the provincial authorities to find out if the family property laws in your province apply to common-law spouses, and whether or not you might have a right to share in your partner's pension if your relationship ends.

The difficulty with sharing a pension on marriage breakdown is that the pension plan member is probably not going to get his pension until many years after you've split up. But his right to the benefit eventually means that it's one of the assets he has and one in which you may be entitled to share. The next problem is figuring out how to put a value on that eventual benefit today. That is, how do you estimate its "present worth," as the actuaries would say?

1) Valuing the benefit. How to calculate the value of the benefit is often one of the most difficult issues to resolve in dividing workplace pensions at divorce. For example, a defined benefit pension plan may provide not just a retirement pension, but also other valuable provisions—sometimes called "ancillary benefits." All these may have to be taken into account in figuring out how much the accumulated pension is worth, before it can be divided between the spouses.

"Ancillary benefits" may be anything from full inflation indexing to generous early retirement benefits, or a surviving-spouse pension that is an "add-on," that is, the plan member's retirement pension is not reduced because a benefit will be paid to his surviving spouse when he dies. (In most plans, a plan member must accept a lower retirement pension if he wants to provide for a surviving spouse, because the pension plan will have to pay benefits for two lifetimes instead of one.) Actuaries may then debate whether or how the value of these additional future benefits should be taken into account in determining the value of the pension today, so that it can be divided when the couple divorces. How to put a value on the various features of a workplace pension plan may become quite controversial. Your lawyer may be able to agree with your spouse's lawyer on what method should be used to value his pension, but in some cases, the judge may have to arbitrate between the views of competing actuaries, yours and his.

Provincial pension laws now prescribe the method or assumptions that have to be used to determine the value of the pension that is to be divided, the procedure to be used in dividing the pension entitlement between the spouses, and the rules for paying out the share of the spouse who will benefit from the division of the pension. But some grey areas still exist. To make life more complicated, public sector workers who work for the federal government, the armed forces, or the RCMP are governed by the Pension Benefits Division Act, which deals with the various aspects of valuing and dividing pension benefits at divorce for employees of the federal government.

In spite of all these laws, significant variations in laws from one jurisdiction to another still create problems, not to mention the difficulties in figuring out exactly what a spouse's pension entitlement may be, and then deciding how to transfer the funds to the beneficiary spouse once that is done.

If you both have your own defined benefit workplace pensions, it may be tempting to say "I'll keep mine and you keep yours." But that's not necessarily in your best interests. One actuary tells of a recent case where the pensions of both husband and wife seemed to be the same. But on closer examination, one was worth $75,000 more than the other because the more valuable one came from a pension plan that had more generous early retirement provisions. A proper evaluation of the pension is important if dividing this key asset is to be fair to both spouses.

Dividing a defined contribution pension plan is much simpler, because these pension plans don't guarantee any particular benefit at retirement. The amount of contributions accumulated in the pension fund can be easily divided between the spouses, without having to worry about how to value the benefits provided by the plan.

2) Mandatory credit-splitting. Manitoba was the only province ever to have had a requirement that the workplace pension be divided 50-50 between the spouses at divorce. The pension laws of this province provided for the share of the non-member spouse to be paid out of the pension plan in a lump sum and the non-member spouse then had to invest the funds in a Locked-In Retirement Account (LIRA). Over the past few years, Manitoba has relaxed its rules on this. For example, since June 1992, Manitoba couples have been able to opt out of the mandatory division of the pension, provided both parties do so in writing after receiving independent legal advice. Manitoba couples have the option of accepting a mandatory 50-50 automatic split, or opting out completely and trading off other assets. If both spouses have pensions and they don't want to opt out of the mandatory division of the pension, they may elect simply to split the difference in the value of the two pensions on a 50-50 basis instead of having to divide each pension in two.

3) How will you get your share of the pension? Once your share of your ex-spouse's pension has been determined under family property laws, just how you'll get access to your share will generally depend on the pension laws of the jurisdiction where his pension is located. Generally, that will be the province where he works. But if he works for a bank, a railway, a telecommunications company, or some other employer under federal jurisdiction—and about 10 percent of the Canadian work force does—access to your share of his pension will depend on federal pension benefits standards legislation. And if he works for a federal or provincial government, his pension may be governed by a special act of Parliament or the provincial legislature.

While the value of his pension may have to be taken into account in determining the total assets that will be shared on divorce, some provinces don't allow pension entitlements built up by one spouse in a workplace pension plan to be divided. In this case, you would have to receive other assets equal in value to your share of the pension. Some provinces don't even address this issue in their pension legislation. In some jurisdictions, even if you're awarded a share of your former spouse's pension at divorce, you may not be able to gain access to it until your spouse retires and starts to receive his pension from his workplace pension plan. At that point, he's supposed to make sure that you get the share you were awarded as part of the divorce settlement. Obviously, that's not a very happy situation. What if you got divorced in your forties, for example, and you were awarded a share in your former husband's pension, but pension legislation in your province doesn't allow your share of the pension to be paid out of his pension plan in a lump sum? That could mean waiting until he retires to get your share. But who wants to depend on his making sure that you receive your share, 20 years or more after your divorce?

What if he doesn't live up to his part of the bargain? You might then be faced with having to take him to court to get your share of the pension. Apart from the cost of doing that, what if he has moved to another jurisdiction by then? How are you going to enforce the pension sharing that the divorce court ordered? Some couples deal with this potential problem by having the pension paid into a trust account with a financial institution, although this is not allowed in Ontario. The trustee is then responsible for seeing that the non-member spouse receives the court-ordered share. However, the administrator of the pension plan is generally obligated to make sure that the non-member spouse's share is paid to her when the member quits or retires (or if the pension plan is terminated) as long as the court order or domestic agreement has been filed with the administrator.

The situation can get even more tricky if your former husband remarries and then dies before retirement. Your right to share in his pension may then be jeopardized because, as a divorced spouse, you may not be entitled to a death benefit if he dies before he gets to retirement. However, your share of his pension awarded when your marriage ended would generally be deducted from the death benefit payable to his second wife. You can also avoid the problem by getting him to agree as part of your divorce settlement to the purchase of a life insurance policy, which will protect your pension entitlement in the event of his death before retirement. With you named as the irrevocable beneficiary, the policy can be for a lump-sum amount equivalent to the value of the benefit you would have received had he lived until retirement.

Under some pension laws, all or part of your share of his pension may be paid out of the pension plan. Depending on the circumstances, the amount may be transferred to another pension plan, for example, if you belong to a different pension plan. Alternatively, your share of his pension may be transferred to a locked-in retirement account (LIRA), or you may use your share of his pension to purchase an immediate or deferred annuity (that is, an annuity where monthly payments will start right away, or one where payments will begin at some date in the future). But generally speaking, you will not be able to receive the amount in cash.

While it may seem advantageous for you to receive a lump-sum payment representing your share of the present value of his accumulated pension benefit, payment of a lump sum today may mean that you'll miss out on any future benefit increases, such as an ad hoc adjustment for inflation, made by the plan sponsor. Other types of arrangements may be possible, depending on the pension laws of the jurisdiction where the pension plan is located. For instance, all or part of your former spouse's pension benefits can be assigned to you, giving you a pension that would be payable as long as your former spouse lives. In effect, this option treats you as if you were a member of the pension plan, so you would benefit from future indexing or ad hoc increases.

Most of these problems are avoided if your former spouse belongs to a defined contribution pension plan. In this kind of plan, dividing the pension is relatively straightforward. Once your share of his accumulated retirement fund is established, it can generally be paid out to you through transferring the amount to a locked-in retirement account (LIRA). For details on LIRAs, see Chapter 5.

4) Restrictions on payouts from pension plans to divorced spouses. Pension laws in almost all jurisdictions do not allow the value of the pension allocated to the divorced spouse—generally the former wife—to exceed 50 percent of the value built up by the pension plan member—generally the former husband—during the marriage. But family property laws may also have special rules on this. In fact, ambiguous or conflicting legislation may sometimes make it impossible for the administrator of the spouse's pension plan to fulfil the judgment ordered by the divorce court. In such cases, the court may have to be petitioned for further guidance.

5) Trading off other assets. Many couples avoid the problems of splitting a defined benefit pension at divorce by trading off other assets in lieu of the pension as part of the divorce settlement. For example, lawyers for both spouses may prepare a net worth statement (assets considered family assets under the law minus liabilities) for each spouse at the beginning and end of the marriage. The increase in each spouse's net worth is then equalized. That is, the spouse with the higher increase in net worth must make an equalization payment to the other spouse. If there are other assets besides the pension plan, the equalization payment can generally be made without affecting the pension. In other words, if the husband is the spouse with the pension, he can retain his full right to the pension, while the wife receives other assets in compensation for giving up her share of the pension.

This may not necessarily be advantageous for the husband, since he may not ever receive the pension—for example, if he dies before retirement. He may then have traded off his right to a share in the couple's assets at the time of divorce for a right to a pension some time in the future, a benefit that he may not live long enough to receive. For the same reasons, from the wife's point of view, a right to a share in the husband's future pension may be less desirable than a right to a share in other assets currently available.

Clearly if the pension is the husband's only asset, such an arrangement wouldn't be feasible. But if there are other assets and they are traded off in lieu of the pension, that may have other financial consequences for you as a woman. Your expectation that you would be able to depend on the financial support of your husband's pension when he retires would no longer be a reality. If you still want to have a pension at retirement, you would have to be responsible for setting aside part of the assets you received in the divorce settlement in lieu of the pension, to provide a benefit for yourself when you get to retirement age. To make matters worse, if you have no earned income, you won't be able to save for retirement by contributing to an RRSP, although payment of a lump sum out of his pension plan could be rolled over tax-free to an RRSP.

6) Getting help to sort it out. As you can see, sharing the workplace pension of your spouse or partner if your relationship ends is highly complex. It's essential that you get your own independent legal advice and that you look for someone who is experienced in pensions. Valuing and dividing accumulated pension benefits is a highly technical exercise, requiring a good actuary. The best way to find the good professional advice you'll need in this situation is to ask around. Friends or people you know, who have been through the same experience, may be able to recommend someone to help you, for example. As Jennie, a divorced mother of five living in Manitoba, told me, "I'm lucky I had a good lawyer who knew what he was doing, otherwise I wouldn't have known I had a right to a share of my husband's pension."

RRSPs and Marriage Breakdown

Funds accumulated in your spouse's RRSP may also be part of the assets you are able to share if your marriage or common-law relationship ends. Again, the amount you may be entitled to from the RRSP of a spouse or partner will depend on the family property laws of the province where you live. And, as noted earlier, in some provinces, common-law spouses are not entitled to share family property if their relationship comes to an end, although there may be support obligations between common-law spouses at the end of their union.

Once it has been determined that you're entitled to a share in your spouse's or partner's RRSP, special rules apply to make the sharing effective. Generally, funds may not be transferred from the RRSP of one spouse to the RRSP of the other. However, an exception is made if the three following conditions are met: you and your spouse or partner were living apart at the time of the transfer; the transfer was made under a written separation agreement or under a decree, order, or judgment of a court; and the transfer was made to settle rights arising out of your marriage on or after the breakdown of your marriage. The same rules apply to RRIFs so that if your spouse's RRSP has already been converted to a RRIF, funds can be transferred directly from your spouse's RRIF to one in your name, or even to an RRSP in your name if the same conditions applying to direct transfers from one spouse's RRSP to the other's are met.

A Surviving-Spouse Pension

If your spouse or partner dies, you will almost certainly be entitled to a surviving-spouse pension, both from the CPP and also from his workplace pension plan if he has one. But changes are anticipated as far as surviving-spouse benefits in the CPP are concerned. Also, you may have previously decided to waive your right to a survivor pension from your spouse's workplace pension plan. For both private and public pension plans, it's important to find out just what benefits you'd get when your spouse dies. Since women generally marry men who are older than they are, and women are likely to live longer than men, a surviving-spouse pension may be a crucial part of your retirement income—especially as you reach your older senior years when you're more likely to be left on your own.

The Spouse's Allowance—A Benefit for Widows

There's one benefit in the first tier of the retirement income system that's directed particularly at widows. If you're between 60 and 64 and are a widow whose annual income was below about $15,500 in 1996, you may be able to claim benefits from the Spouse's Allowance program, although the maximum benefit of about $775 a month is payable only to a widow in this age group who has virtually no income at all. The thresholds and rates for this program are adjusted every quarter in line with inflation.

You can also get the Spouse's Allowance, described in detail in Chapter 4, if you're married to a low-income pensioner and your joint annual income as a couple is below about $21,000 (at 1996 rates). As a widow, though, your eligibility for the program is based on your income alone. It doesn't matter how long you've been a widow or how much income your spouse had when he was alive; once you reach age 60, you may qualify for benefits if your income is below the threshold.

The Canada Pension Plan

As noted in Chapter 4, the CPP pays a benefit to the surviving spouse when a contributor dies. The amount of the benefit will depend on your age and whether you have dependent children. If you're 65 or older when your spouse dies, you'll receive a benefit equivalent to 60 percent of his retirement pension, or 60 percent of the retirement pension he would have received had he turned 65 on the day of his death, up to a maximum of $436 a month (at 1996 rates). (In this chapter, the monthly amounts payable under various government programs have been rounded to the nearest dollar.) Younger surviving spouses get less, as explained earlier. And surviving spouses under age 35 don't qualify for CPP survivor benefits unless these spouses are disabled or have dependent children. However, if your spouse contributed to the Quebec Pension Plan, you may be entitled to a surviving spouse pension when he dies, even if you're under the age of 35, but only if the QPP is responsible for the administration of your benefit—that is, you are living in Quebec, or he contributed to both the QPP and the CPP, or only to the QPP. The QPP pays survivor benefits to surviving spouses under age 35 regardless of whether or not they are disabled or have dependent children.

Because the amount of your spouse's CPP retirement pension will depend on how much and for how long he has paid into the plan, your survivor benefit will also vary according to these same considerations. Most women are above the age of 65 when they start receiving a surviving-spouse pension. But although the maximum CPP survivor benefit for this age group in 1996 was $436 a month, the average benefit being received by women who started to get their survivor pensions in August 1996 was only about $290 a month.

For you to be eligible for a surviving-spouse benefit at all, your spouse must have contributed to the CPP for at least three years. But if his CPP "contributory period"—that is, the total span of time during his life when he was entitled to contribute to the CPP—is longer than 10 years, he must have contributed in at least one-third of the calendar years in his contributory period or for 10 calendar years, whichever is less.

The CPP "contributory period" is the period of time from the age of 18 or January 1, 1966, whichever is later, to the date when you start receiving your CPP retirement pension, or the age of 70, or the date of your death. If your spouse is now in his sixties, for example, his contributory period would be about 30 years. If he died when he was 70, he would have to have contributed to the plan for at least 10 years for you to be entitled to a surviving-spouse benefit. If he was receiving a CPP disability pension at any time during his contributory period, that time can be removed from the contributory period because you don't have to contribute to the CPP while you are getting disability benefits.

All this may be easier to understand if we try an example. Suppose your husband was born in 1967 and dies in 2012 at the age of 45. He was working and contributing to the CPP from the age of 21. His "contributory period" would normally be from 18 to 65. But since he died at 45, his contributory period ends in 2012, at his death. In other words, it's 27 years (45 – 18). (For the sake of simplicity, we'll assume these are calendar years.) If he received CPP disability benefits for five of those years, let's say, his contributory period would be only 22 years.

Since his contributory period is more than 10 years, he must have contributed for at least one-third of those years or for 10 years, whichever is less. Assuming he did not receive disability benefits during those years, one-third of his contributory period is nine years. And he contributed for 24 years (from the age of 21 to the age of 45). That means he met the conditions, and you'll get your survivor benefit, depending on your age as described below.

The calculation of CPP surviving spouse benefits for younger spouses is incredibly complicated. You should also be aware that these provisions of the CPP are under review as part of the proposed CPP reforms now being considered. Watch for changes in the near future. You can always check with your local Income Security Programs office for an update. Under the existing system, if you're aged 45 to 54 when your spouse dies, your survivor benefit will consist of a flat-rate portion, which in 1996 was about $127 a month, plus 37.5 percent of what CPP calls your spouse's "calculated" retirement pension—that is, the retirement pension he would have received had he been 65 when he died. The maximum CPP survivor benefit in 1996 for spouses under the age of 65 was roughly $400 a month.

If you're under 45 when he dies, and you are disabled or raising a dependent child, your survivor benefit will be calculated in the same way. If you're between 35 and 45 when he dies, you're not raising any dependent children, or you're not disabled, your survivor benefit will be calculated as described, but some money will be subtracted from the pension. The amount subtracted will be $\frac{1}{120}$ of the benefit for each month you were under the age of 45 when your spouse died. This pension will be paid to you for the rest of your life.

As noted above, if you are under 35 when your spouse dies, you can only get a surviving-spouse benefit if you are disabled or if you have dependent children. Assuming you qualify, the benefit is based on a flat-rate component and the 37.5 percent of your spouse's "calculated" retirement pension, as noted above. If you no longer meet the conditions—for example, your children are no longer dependent on you—your surviving-spouse pension will be suspended. However, it would be reinstated if you became disabled, and it will be reinstated once you reach 65. At that point, the benefit is recalculated, based on your deceased spouse's contribution record. For instance, suppose: he had contributed at the maximum rate during his contributory period; he met the condition that he had contributed for at least three years; and he also contributed for at least 10 years or one-third of his contributory period. You would then be entitled to the maximum surviving-spouse benefit in effect at the time you turn 65.

The CPP surviving-spouse pension is paid to the person who, at the time of the contributor's death, is the legal or common-law spouse of the deceased contributor. But a common-law spouse, in order to qualify for a surviving-spouse benefit, must have been living with the contributor when that person died. As noted before, a common-law spouse is a person of the opposite sex with whom you have been living in a conjugal relationship for at least one year. If you are a separated, legal spouse and your former spouse has no cohabiting common-law spouse at the time of his death, you may still qualify for a CPP surviving-spouse benefit. This can also get quite complicated. For example, suppose you were legally separated from your husband, and he established a common-law relationship with someone else. But let's say, by the time he dies, he had split up with his common-law spouse. Because he has no "spouse" living with him at the time of his death, you would be entitled to the surviving-spouse benefit, because you are still legally married to him. Of course, his common-law spouse may have applied for a division of credits when their common-law union ended, so the survivor benefits you would get would be based on his share of the pension credits after that credit-split had been made.

Surviving-spouse benefits from the CPP are not paid automatically; you must apply for them. As the surviving spouse, that's your responsibility and you should apply as soon as possible after your spouse's or partner's death. You could lose benefits if you delay, because the CPP can only make back payments for up to 12 months. You can get an application form from your local Income Security Programs office, listed in the phone book under Human Resources Development Canada. You should also note that if you are widowed for a second time, you will not be able to get two surviving-spouse benefits, one from each former spouse. Only one surviving-spouse pension will be paid and it will be the larger of the two.

If you remarry, you will continue to get your surviving-spouse benefit. Prior to 1987 these benefits ceased if the surviving spouse remarried. If you previously lost a survivor benefit because of remarriage, you may want to contact your nearest Income Security Programs office to have the benefit reinstated.

Once you apply for your surviving-spouse benefit, it may take up to 12 weeks to process your application. But the benefit can be paid for the month after your spouse's death, so your payment will be backdated to that point—as long as it's not more than 12 months ago. If your circumstances change, you should notify the CPP right away. If you get benefits to which you're not entitled, you will be required to pay them back. For instance, if you're under 35 when your spouse dies and you claim a survivor benefit because you still have dependent children, you won't be able to continue getting the benefit once the children are no longer dependent on you.

As noted earlier, if you have both your own retirement pension and a surviving-spouse pension from the CPP, the most you can get from these two benefits combined is equivalent to the maximum CPP retirement pension, which in 1996 was $727 a month.

Workplace Pension Plans

In the past, few pension plans provided benefits for surviving spouses when pension plan members died. Even where such benefits were available, the plan member had to accept a lower retirement benefit himself in order to provide an ongoing benefit for his widow when he died—assuming he died after retirement. Many plan members opted against the surviving-spouse benefit because they wanted to have a higher retirement pension while they were still alive. Since most pension plan members are men, and since most surviving spouses are women, this meant that many women whose husbands had private workplace pensions were left without benefits when their husbands died.

Pension reforms, implemented during the 1980s, have made surviving-spouse benefits mandatory for private workplace pension plans whether the plan member dies before or after retirement. Now, the surviving spouse of a pension plan contributor must receive a pension of at least 60 percent of the retirement benefit being paid to the contributor, unless both spouses waive that right in writing. Decisions about a post-retirement surviving-spouse benefit will usually be made at retirement, when various options are presented to the pension plan member. It may be tempting to sign away your right to a survivor benefit because your spouse will get a higher retirement pension if you do. But unless some other provisions have been made for your financial support after he's gone, it's not a wise move.

Surviving-spouse benefits in workplace pension plans generally can be paid to a spouse who was legally married or one who was in a common-law relationship. But if you are separated from your husband, and at the time of his death he has already formed a common-law relationship with someone else, his common-law spouse will be considered his surviving spouse for the purposes of survivor benefits from his workplace pension plan.

More and more workplace pension plans are now covering same-sex couples, so that if a plan member dies, surviving-spouse benefits will be paid to her surviving same-sex partner. As mentioned earlier, all workplace pension plans must be registered with Revenue Canada for tax purposes. Because the Income Tax Act does not recognize same-sex relationships, Revenue Canada will not register a workplace pension plan that includes coverage of same-sex relationships for tax purposes. This situation is being challenged as being contrary to the Charter of Rights, in litigation that is wending its way through the court system. In the meantime, employers voluntarily offering surviving-spouse pension benefits for same-sex partners may get around the problem by putting in special funding for these benefits.

Choosing the Surviving-Spouse Option

A booklet from the Pension Commission of Ontario gives the example of Frances and Frank, who are reviewing Frank's retirement option statement and are faced with choosing one of the following three options:

- A single life annuity, with no guarantee period, that will pay Frank $1,000 a month as long as he lives. This is the kind of pension an unmarried pension plan member might expect to get. It pays a monthly benefit for the rest of the plan member's life. But, because there is no guarantee of receiving payments for at least a certain number of years, Frances will get nothing when Frank dies. He could die the day after starting his monthly annuity payments, or he could live for another 15 years, but his benefits will continue for his life only.

- A single life annuity with a guarantee period of 10 years that will pay Frank $930 a month. If Frank dies within the 10-year period after his retirement, Frances will receive the same monthly payment as Frank was getting until the 10 years are up. After that, she gets nothing. If Frank lives for 15 or even 20 years after he retires, he'll still go on getting the payments, because they continue for the rest of his life. But, because only 10 years of payments are guaranteed, if Frank lives for longer than 10 years, Frances will get nothing when he dies.
- A 60 percent joint and survivor annuity (in plain English, a joint pension that continues to pay benefits to the surviving spouse when the contributor spouse dies) that will pay Frank $850 a month during his lifetime, and then go on paying $510 a month (60 percent of $850) to Frances (after Frank's death) for the rest of her life.

If Frank and Frances do their planning as a couple—which, of course, is what they should be doing—they will choose the third option, because it pays a benefit to the surviving spouse, even though it will give them $150 ($1,000 – $850) less each month while Frank is alive.

What Happens If He Dies before Retirement?

While it's easy to see the advantages of choosing to have a percentage of your spouse's pension continue to be paid to you after he's gone, if he dies before he even gets to retirement, you will be in a different situation. Generally speaking, instead of getting a monthly pension that's a percentage of what your spouse would have received, you'll probably get a lump-sum payment that represents the value today (which actuaries call "the commuted value") of the pension your spouse had accumulated when he died. In effect, this represents the value now of the series of payments he would have received in the future. (This only applies to defined benefit pension plans, because, as you'll remember, defined contribution plans don't promise any particular benefit in the future.)

Your exact position may depend on what province you live in and when that province's current pension legislation came into force. In Ontario, for instance, before January 1, 1987, there was no legislated requirement for surviving spouses to receive a payment if the spouse who belonged to the pension plan died before retirement. That means if you live in Ontario and your spouse dies before reaching retirement, you have no right to the benefits he accumulated before January 1, 1987, unless the pension plan he belonged to specifically provides for it. But if he was contributing to the plan himself, you are entitled to get back any contributions he made to the plan before January 1, 1987, plus interest. This refund will usually be paid to you as a lump sum.

Vested benefits earned after December 31, 1986 (vesting was explained in Chapter 5) will be paid to you, the surviving spouse, as a death benefit. If he belonged to a defined contribution pension plan, you're entitled to get back both his contributions and those of his employer, plus interest. The amount will be paid to you in a lump sum. If he belonged to a defined benefit pension plan, you'll get back the commuted value (the value today) of your spouse's accumulated pension—either as a lump-sum payment, or as an immediate or deferred annuity. That is, an annuity that will start making monthly payments to you immediately, or will start the payments at a later (or deferred) date. In Ontario, if you don't choose which option you want within 90 days of your spouse's death, the administrator of his pension plan may decide to pay your death benefit as a pension.

If your spouse's pension wasn't vested when he died, you're entitled to get back anything he contributed to the plan with interest. The refund is payable as a lump sum.

Under the Ontario pension laws, if the pension plan member is vested (that is, he has been in the pension plan long enough to be entitled to the promised benefits at retirement), the spouse living with him at the time of death is automatically the beneficiary, unless the spouse has waived that entitlement in writing. Similar rules apply in other provinces.

Providing a Pension for Yourself after Your Spouse Dies

There are several ways in which you might use a lump-sum payment from your spouse's pension plan to provide for your own future financial security, depending on your age. The best way is probably to roll it over into an RRSP, which Revenue Canada will allow you to do tax-free. You could also use the lump sum to purchase an immediate or deferred annuity for yourself—that is, an annuity that will give you a regular monthly income, starting immediately or at some point in the future.

Check the Rules in Your Province

As mentioned earlier, pension legislation varies from one jurisdiction to another, although pension regulators have tried to co-ordinate their legislative changes and to make sure provisions are consistent from one jurisdiction to another. Contact the pension commission, if there is one, in your province, or the Ministry of Labour or Employment Standards Branch, for information about what pension laws apply in your province. But you also need to check carefully to see what provisions are made in your spouse's pension plan for payment of benefits to a surviving spouse—especially if he dies before retirement.

RRSPs and RRIFs

The treatment of RRSPs and RRIFs when the holder dies is very simple. Effectively, the surviving spouse inherits them tax-free. There's some question as to whether the spouse needs to be named as beneficiary on the RRSP document and in the will as well. To be sure, you and your spouse may want to talk to a lawyer to make sure that the RRSPs or RRIFs are set up in the right way, so that the funds pass to the survivor without any hassles when one of you dies.

When your spouse dies, his RRSP can be rolled over to you and it then becomes your plan; you may continue making contributions to this plan, within your own contribution limit. Special forms have to be filled out to effect the transfer. Your local tax office can give you further information.

Similar rules apply to RRIFs. In fact, the minimum withdrawals from these plans can be calculated based on the age of the younger spouse, which is often the wife. When the first spouse dies, the surviving spouse becomes the "annuitant" of the plan—that is, assuming you're the surviving spouse, you take over the plan and continue making the withdrawals. You have to include these amounts in your income and pay tax on them as they're withdrawn.

CHAPTER 8

OTHER WAYS OF SAVING FOR RETIREMENT

Your RRSP is an ideal way to save for retirement—especially if you don't have a workplace pension plan. But if you don't have earned income, you won't be entitled to make an RRSP contribution. On the other hand, it may be that you're entitled to make an RRSP contribution, but you can't afford to because your earnings are too low, and you just can't find the spare cash. You may even be in the fortunate position of being a high-income earner, who would like to save more than the maximum amount you're allowed to put into your RRSP each year. In all these situations, there may still be ways to save and build up a retirement fund for yourself. This chapter will examine ways in which you may be able to get extra cash to save or invest, how you can invest outside an RRSP, and how you might tap into other sources of financial support for your senior years.

How to Be Financially Independent, though Married

Marriage has an impact on your earnings. In the general scheme of things, marriage tends to lower the earnings of women and improve the earnings of men. If you're married, setting aside your own savings may be difficult enough, even if you have a paying job outside your home. If you're a full-time homemaker, it may be next to impossible to put aside your own savings. Does it really matter? After all, you and your partner get along well, you've planned together for your retirement, you're both equally involved in managing the family finances and doing the investing, and you expect to have enough to replace your joint pre-retirement income so you can live comfortably in your old age. If you can say honestly that all those statements are true, you're probably in good shape. "What's mine is yours" may be something that you hear quite often, so why worry?

Apart from the fact that it might feel good to have a bit of economic autonomy, there's also the possibility that this happy state of affairs won't last forever. The government's proposal to base the new Seniors Benefit on family income, for example, has come in for quite a bit of criticism from married women. For many of them, the change will take away the only pension they have ever received in their own name as a right and without reference to their husbands. Now is probably the time to emphasize, yet again, that it's vital for you to get involved in planning for your own financial future. Even if your state of married bliss continues until you reach a ripe old age, you will almost certainly be left alone eventually—probably as a widow.

Your Access to Financial Resources

Some women, of course, are not even interested in finding out where the money comes from and where it goes. Like Brenda, whom I mentioned earlier, they have no idea what money their husbands make, what investments their husbands have, and what plans their husbands made for retirement. That's a dangerous state to be in. Over the years, many women have told me how devastated they were when their husbands died, or when their marriage ended. One woman said, "I didn't even know where his bank accounts were. I didn't know what investments he had, and when I found out, I didn't know how to handle them." Having to cope with a serious financial crisis like this at a time when you're facing the shock of bereavement is almost unbearable. But it's also avoidable, if you resolve now to get involved.

Learning how to be assertive may also be key to your financial security in retirement, but for some reason, many women seem to find this a tough one. Let me tell you about my friend Dorothy, who was married to Brian. Brian had a high-powered sales job with a major multinational corporation. He was forever wining and dining clients in fancy restaurants on his expense account. His salary was paid into a Swiss bank account—yes, really! Dorothy had no idea how much money he made. And because it was her second marriage and she had custody of the two children from her first marriage, Brian expected Dorothy to pay all expenses related to the children, even though her first husband refused to pay her any child support. Dorothy was also expected to pay half the mortgage and half of all the other household expenses. Struggling to raise the children, without much help from Brian, as well as holding down a modestly paid teaching job so she could pay her "share" of the expenses was incredibly stressful for Dorothy. It's a wonder she was even able to keep going. Why didn't she leave him? Well, love does strange things to people, I guess. The point of the story is that, even though Brian and Dorothy's joint income was way above average, Dorothy did not have equal access to the financial resources that should have been coming into the household. And yes, she did leave him eventually. But by the time that happened, she was so browbeaten, she was glad to see the back of him. She wasn't able to stand up to him in the divorce negotiations either. To make matters worse, the lump-sum payment he told the court he would deposit in her bank account never materialized and nothing was done about it.

Financially, her divorce settlement was a disaster for her. Now she's retired and living in very modest circumstances, struggling to get by on a small teacher's pension and her CPP.

Economists generally assume that the family is the basic unit of economic decision making and consumption. Implicitly, they assume that income coming into the family is pooled between all family members and that they all share equally in decisions about spending it—what economists like to call "household consumption." That's also the basic assumption of government programs that provide benefits based on family income. For instance, your right to the new Seniors Benefit will depend on your and your spouse's income together, so the implicit assumption is that you have equal access to the money coming into the household. It wasn't true in Dorothy's case. And there's increasing evidence that it's not true in a lot of households—especially in those where there is wife abuse. In such families, economic abuse also seems to be common. It can take the form of forcing the wife to ask for money, giving the wife an allowance, taking the wife's money away, and not letting the wife know about or have access to family income.

The Ontario Fair Tax Commission, which had a three-year mandate to study tax reform in the province and reported at the end of 1993, set up a working group to study women and taxation. The working group pointed out that the way in which resources are allocated among family members seems to be much more complex than simply sharing everything. All kinds of arrangements exist—as you'll know if you've ever asked other couples how they share their income, divide up expenses, and who pays for what. Other studies have suggested that the financial bonds between spouses may start to unravel long before they get to the divorce court. In fact, it may be one of the early signs the marriage is in trouble. Failure to provide financial support is often one of the grounds cited for divorce.

Asserting Yourself Financially

If you're totally, or even partially, dependent on your spouse or partner for financial support, it may be difficult to preserve some financial autonomy and save for your old age. Short of squirreling away some of your housekeeping money, what can you do? Here are a few suggestions.

- Start by insisting that you and your spouse or partner sit down together to discuss your financial situation and develop a long-term retirement plan.
- Make sure the plan includes an adequate retirement income for you when he is no longer around—through surviving-spouse benefits from his workplace pension plan, a life insurance policy, your spousal RRSP, a rollover of his RRSPs (for which you should be named as beneficiary), investments, and whatever else he has.
- As part of this process, make sure you are aware of all the financial assets you both have—bank accounts, investments, life insurance policies, pension plans, RRSPs, and so on—as well as other property, such as real estate, a business, and collectibles that may be worth something. You need to know where they are, the amounts involved, who is named as beneficiary, and what will happen when he dies.
- Whether you have your own income, or he is the only one bringing home a paycheque, plan that a certain amount of your joint income each month will be yours alone, for you to invest or save. It could be a flat dollar amount or a percentage of your joint income. Once you decide, make sure you review the amount regularly—say, every year, when you should also do an assessment of how you're doing financially, both individually and as a couple.
- If you're not entitled to contribute to an RRSP because you have little or no earned income of your own, develop a savings or

investment plan for yourself. You can set up a regular monthly contribution of as little as $50 and put that into a good mutual fund and start building up a retirement nest egg for yourself. The amount can be increased later, when you can afford it. Further ideas will be discussed in the next chapter.

- If you get an unexpected windfall (for example, your Aunt Minnie dies and leaves you a couple of thousand dollars, your parents give you money for your birthday, or you win the lottery), try to add it to your personal retirement fund. Even small amounts—money you made at this year's garage sale, for instance—can be added to the pot.
- Get involved in your spousal RRSP, if your spouse is contributing to one for you. Know how much is in your plan and how it is invested. Insist on being involved in decisions on how to invest the funds. If you feel you're not confident enough to assert yourself in this way, take some courses, do some reading, and boost your self-confidence by making it your business to develop some expertise.

These may seem like little things, but the money in your fund will soon mount up and you'll have the satisfaction of knowing that not only are you building a retirement fund for yourself, but you're also establishing your own economic autonomy.

Can You Save after Divorce?

The possibility of sharing in a spouse's pension at divorce or marriage breakdown has already been discussed. Remember, too, that common-law spouses may not have the same rights as legally married spouses to a share in family assets at the end of their relationship. What if you find yourself with a lump-sum settlement instead of a share in his pension? What if there is no pension to be shared? What if you find you're not entitled to a share in the family assets anyway?

Will a divorce make it more difficult to provide a secure financial future for yourself? That's a distinct possibility. If you think divorce or the end of a long-term relationship may be looming in your future, try to think through the financial aspects of your situation so you can minimize the damage.

Apart from sharing his CPP credits, getting funds from his workplace pension plan, or money from his RRSP, there are a couple of other ways in which a divorce or marriage breakdown might help—or perhaps hinder—your ability to save for your own retirement. The termination of the relationship could result in your being awarded maintenance or spousal support, or you could get a lump-sum settlement.

Spousal and Child Support

To be honest, your chances of being awarded spousal support on divorce or marriage breakdown are not that great. And even if you're lucky enough to get it, the amount may be so meagre you may have to review your retirement savings program and make adjustments. If there are children involved, the courts will almost certainly award child support to the custodial parent. Awards of spousal support are much less likely. Courts have often taken the position that women can just go out to work and support themselves, even if they've been out of the paid labour force for years. I once had to testify as an expert witness in a divorce case where a wealthy husband didn't want to pay spousal support to his 50-year-old former wife. During their marriage, he had taken the position that no wife of his was going to go out to work. She had married him straight out of high school and had never been in the paid work force. Now that they were divorcing, he argued that she was perfectly capable of going out and finding a job. The judge seemed quite taken aback when I testified that, with no skills and no recent work experience, she would be lucky if she could find a job at all. The best she might hope for was some kind of menial work at minimum wage. The judge eventually awarded her quite generous spousal support payments, but it was touch and go for a while.

Canada's Divorce Act sets out four objectives for spousal support:

1. Recognition of the economic advantages and disadvantages to the spouses arising from the marriage breakdown;
2. The apportionment between the spouses of the financial consequences arising from the care of children;
3. The relief of financial hardship; and
4. The promotion of self-sufficiency.

It's that last one that seems to play a big role in many court decisions. An evaluation of the Divorce Act, prepared for the federal Department of Justice in 1990, noted that spousal support was rarely requested and rarely granted. A request for spousal support was indicated in only 16 percent of the 1,478 divorce files reviewed, and in just 19 percent of the 1,210 cases where there were dependent children. Other studies for the Department of Justice have identified some trends in divorce settlements as far as support orders are concerned. Courts were likely to make orders for permanent spousal support for women who had been traditional homemakers during their marriage, but the level of support is generally quite low. Women with dependent children from medium-length marriages (say, 10 to 15 years) were less likely to receive spousal support, and if they did, it would be for limited periods and at very low levels. Even after the landmark 1992 decision by the Supreme Court of Canada in the Moge case, which was discussed earlier, it seems that spousal support orders have increased only marginally.

Many judges apparently believe that a property settlement at the time of divorce is enough to compensate a woman for the economic disadvantage she faces at divorce. Despite the Supreme Court's comments on the permanent impact marriage can have on a woman's earning power, few courts seem willing to take that into account when it comes to awarding spousal support. Getting a lump-sum payment that represents your share of the family property probably won't give you an income to live on—especially if the family home accounts for a big chunk of the assets. However, as mentioned earlier, there may be support obligations between common-law spouses in some provinces, even though the provincial family property laws don't give them the right to share in family assets.

Some courts do seem to have taken a stand, though. For example, in a 1987 divorce case (*Horn v. Horn*, [1987] 11 R.F.L. (3d) 23, 49 Man.R. (2d) 301 at 303-304 (C.A.) aff'd [1987], 48 Man.R. (2d) 142 [Q.B.]), decided by the Manitoba Court of Appeal, the court said, "There are many factors connected with a marriage which contribute to the ability of a spouse to earn an income. Due to the support which one spouse receives from the other (support which is not necessarily financial), one spouse may have gained advantages such as educational opportunities or job experience. The other may have been prejudiced in his or her income earning capacity by reason of time spent away from the work force attending to the comforts of the other or of children of the marriage. When the couple separates, it is unreasonable to say in every case that each must be financially independent thereafter . . . the prejudice to the income earning capacity of one (spouse) resulting from the marriage may last a lifetime."

Whether or not you're granted spousal support when your marriage or common-law relationship ends, if you also have custody of the children, inadequate child support payments (or the failure of your former spouse to make the court-ordered payments) may hamper your ability to save for your retirement, because you'll have the burden of trying to make up the difference from your own earnings or financial resources. Federal and provincial governments have introduced measures to try to improve the level of child support awards and to make sure that they are paid. But some provincial governments are now cutting back on their maintenance enforcement programs as part of the current push to cut government spending.

On the positive side, changes in the tax treatment of support payments have been announced that should be helpful to those who receive maintenance or child support. Until recently, the person making these payments—usually the husband—could deduct them from his income for tax purposes, while the custodial parent who received them—usually the wife—had to include them in her income and pay tax on them. In theory, this system was supposed to encourage non-custodial parents to comply with their court-ordered support obligations to their children and to enable them to make higher payments because they could claim a tax deduction for the entire amount paid. The idea of giving tax incentives to persuade divorced fathers to support their children doesn't seem to have been very effective, since more than 70 percent of court-ordered payments were in default in some provinces. And, of course, custodial parents, who also contributed to the financial support of their children, didn't get a tax deduction for the amounts they spent. Nor did fathers (or mothers) who continued to live with their families in ongoing marriages and provided financial support for their children. In the 1996 federal budget, the Finance Minister announced that child support paid pursuant to an agreement or court order made on or after May 1, 1997, will not have to be included in the income of the recipient for tax purposes, nor will it be deductible for the person who pays it. The changes will not affect child support orders made prior to May 1, 1997, unless and until the child support order is revised.

It goes without saying that many divorces and custody arrangements are settled amicably and many husbands and fathers are happy to meet their financial obligations to their former spouses and to their children. But the thought of having to cope with a hassle over support payments is obviously depressing. Apart from what it might do to your ability to support yourself and your children financially, it could really put a dent in your efforts to save and add to your retirement nest egg. But the problems are not insurmountable, especially if you are financially aware and you plan carefully.

With this kind of awareness and planning, you should be able to avoid the position in which Agnes finds herself. A 47-year-old divorced mother of two, she earns about $17,000 a year. She didn't get any child support payments when she was divorced, about 16 years ago, and she doesn't know if she received a share of her husband's CPP credits. She has invested in an RRSP, but she doesn't know how much money she has in her plan. And, while she belongs to a pension plan at work, she doesn't know what kind of plan it is. But, typical Canadian that she is—and despite the total absence of planning for her financial future—Agnes is optimistic about her retirement. She's looking forward to retirement, and she's counting on her workplace pension and her RRSP to provide her with enough to live on. What's more, Agnes is hoping to retire in just three years' time, when she's 50.

Contrast Agnes with Betty, whom I spoke to a couple of years ago. Betty had been divorced about as long as Agnes has been, but Betty had planned and saved, so she had good reason to be optimistic. Betty, 54 years old at the time, had four grown children. She did get child support after her divorce, but she said that because she stayed in the family home with the children, she had to pay it back to reimburse her husband for his share in the home. She didn't get a share of her husband's CPP credits. But when we talked, she had about $200,000 in her RRSP. Of course, it was easier for Betty than for Agnes to save, because Betty earned $45,000 a year. But she also understood her workplace pension plan, and seemed to have planned carefully for her retirement. She was planning to retire at 65 and was looking forward to a retirement free of financial worries. She'll probably achieve it, too.

Your Share of the Family Assets

Saving after divorce is obviously much easier if you are awarded a share of the family assets. You may be able to continue living in the family home, like Betty did, or you may acquire a lump sum representing your share of the assets. Depending on the amount you receive, there's potential here for you to set some of the money aside to secure your financial well-being in old age. What's the best way to do that? It depends on how much you have, how you feel about investments, how long you have to go until retirement, and whether you will have other sources of retirement income, such as a workplace pension or RRSP.

Receiving a lump-sum payment from a former spouse as part of a court-ordered settlement on divorce or dissolution of a common-law relationship has no immediate tax consequences. Your spouse is not permitted to deduct the amount for tax purposes and you don't have to declare it as income. But no provisions exist to let you roll over the amount into an RRSP. Of course, if you are entitled to make an RRSP contribution in the year you receive the funds, you could use part of the money to contribute to your RRSP within your contribution limit. You might even invest the money temporarily and use part of it each year to contribute to your RRSP. But receiving a lump-sum payment as part of a settlement on marriage breakdown does not entitle you to additional RRSP contribution room.

The Widow's Mite

It seems society traditionally views widows as poor and vulnerable. You may remember the biblical story of the widow who cast her two mites, which was all the money she had, into the treasury. The widow's mite—which, at least according to the Oxford dictionary, was "a Flemish copper coin of small value"—has come to symbolize the traditional poverty of widows down the ages. It's true, many widows don't have much money, even today. But even poor widows sometimes inherit a lump-sum payment if their spouse or partner has made them the beneficiary of his life insurance policy. This may be another potential source of retirement savings for you. Even if you also get a surviving-spouse pension from the CPP or from his workplace pension plan, the proceeds of his life insurance policy might be invested to provide additional retirement income for you.

Life Insurance

While more women are buying life insurance, the majority of individual policies are still purchased by men. As well, many men are covered under group life insurance policies provided by their employers. About 67 percent of those insured under individual life insurance policies and 73 percent of those insured under group life insurance policies are men. More than half the amounts paid out under both kinds of policies go to the wives of the individuals insured.

But don't get your hopes up without knowing the facts. Overall, statistics from the Canadian Life and Health Association show that the majority of policies on which death benefits were paid out were for relatively small amounts of money. In an analysis of death benefits paid out in March 1993, the association reported that 75 percent of benefits paid out under individual life insurance policies and 66 percent of those paid under group life insurance policies were for amounts of less than $10,000. The association said this reflected the fact that more than half these policies had been issued more than 30 years ago. Only 3 percent of benefits paid out under individual policies and 4 percent of benefits paid under group policies were for amounts of $100,000 or more.

Make it a priority to discuss life insurance with your spouse or partner and make sure you are provided for. But make sure, too, that you know how much insurance coverage there is. You should also be aware that, while your spouse or partner may have life insurance coverage through his work, that coverage may be reduced significantly, or even come to an end, when he retires. It may be possible for him to keep up the policy by continuing to pay the premiums himself, converting it to an individual life insurance policy, but this is something you'll need to look into. If you're counting on life insurance as a key part of your financial support after he's gone, make sure you have the coverage you need. The same considerations apply to those in a same-sex relationship.

Benefits you receive under a life insurance policy as a result of the death of your spouse or partner are not taxable, since they are specifically exempt from taxation under the law.

Inheriting Financial Assets

You may inherit other assets if your spouse or partner dies. Apart from RRSPs or RRIFs, which can be passed on to legal or common-law (but not same-sex) surviving spouses, who then become the annuitants (or holders) of these plans, any of your spouse's investments, bank accounts, and other financial assets may become yours as a result of widowhood. These assets can generally be passed on to a surviving spouse without tax consequences. It could mean you would then acquire an investment portfolio, which may provide you with an income as well as with a way of saving for your old age. How you would deal with this will depend on how much you receive, and how comfortable you are with handling investments. But, if you've followed the advice given earlier about being involved in the financial planning and management of your joint financial resources with your spouse or partner, inheriting financial assets as a result of his death should come as no surprise. You would also have discussed how you would manage these assets if you should be left alone as a widow, and whether or not you'll seek help from a money manager or other financial professional. Estate planning is another area that many couples seem to neglect, but it is vitally important to ensure your own future financial security, as well as to avoid having to go through a financial trauma at the same time as you're trying to cope with the emotional loss of your spouse or partner.

Investing a Lump-Sum Settlement

If you receive a lump-sum settlement when your relationship ends, whether through divorce, the death of your spouse or partner, the breakdown of a common-law relationship, or for any other reason, setting up an investment portfolio with the money is an option to be considered seriously. And if you're not an experienced investor, you may want to get some professional advice on how to do this. How to get financial planning advice was explained in Chapter 3. You may also want to take another look at the section on investing defined contribution pension plans in Chapter 5. To repeat, there are no hard and fast rules about investments. It's up to you to do your homework and decide what mix of investments suits your particular circumstances and comfort level. The younger you are, the more adventurous you can be, because there's still time to recover from any investment mistakes before you need to start tapping into your retirement fund. But, unless you're a really experienced investor, it's never a good idea to put a lot of money into "hot tips" or investment fads.

Don't let yourself get talked into putting your money into some kind of investment you don't understand, just because someone at a retirement planning seminar told you it was a good idea. And don't be tempted to buy a particular stock because your next-door neighbour tells you it's a sure-fire bet. A bet may be exactly what it is, and you'll probably lose. Over many years of answering readers' questions about personal finance in my column in *The Financial Post*, I received a lot of letters from people who had followed investment fads, without really understanding what they were getting into. They were writing because they wanted to get out and didn't know what to do or how to do it. I heard about everything from limited partnerships for run-down condominiums in Florida, to shipping containers and Lloyds' "Names" (investors who formed syndicates to underwrite insurance and lost millions of dollars when they couldn't meet the insurance claims). And I could paper several houses with copies of old stock certificates for worthless penny mining stocks that readers sent in.

One general rule you may find useful if you're an inexperienced investor is that as you get older, you'll probably want to be more conservative in your approach to investing. That's because the nearer you are to retirement, the less time there is to recoup any losses you might sustain on your investments. You may also want to take this approach if the thought of going anywhere near the stock market makes you break out in a cold sweat. As mentioned before, if you have that problem, a good balanced mutual fund could be an option for you. But even the idea of a mutual fund makes some people tremble.

For the really nervous investor, many financial advisers suggest spreading your portfolio over a range of Guaranteed Investment Certificates (GICs) with different maturities. You might start out by putting 20 percent in one-year GICs, 20 percent in two-year GICs, 20 percent in three-year GICs, 20 percent in four-year GICs, and 20 percent in GICs maturing in five years. As each set of GICs mature, you roll over the funds into a new GIC maturing in five years. In this way, one-fifth of your portfolio matures each year and can be rolled over. The advantage of this strategy is that it gives you some protection against interest rate movements. For instance, suppose you invested your entire lump-sum amount in five-year GICs when interest rates were 10 percent. When your fund matures in five years, rates may have dropped to 5 percent and you would be faced with having to reinvest the entire amount at a much lower rate of interest.

Reinvesting at a rate that is so much lower would mean the earnings on your investment would drop precipitously. By spreading your funds over different maturities, you'll balance off low and high interest rates, giving you a better average rate of return.

The disadvantage of this strategy, though, is that your rate of return is likely to be very modest, compared with what you might have achieved on a balanced mutual fund or blue chip stocks, as explained in Chapter 6. If you're still not confident in your investment ability, the solution might be to try the GIC strategy for the time being, and resolve to improve your investment knowledge and expertise, so you can set up a more diversified portfolio of investments that will give you a better rate of return in the long run. Of course, the GIC strategy would only be worthwhile if you have enough money to invest. Financial institutions generally require a minimum investment for GICs, which can range anywhere from $1,000 to $5,000 and occasionally $10,000. If you have only $10,000 from the proceeds of a life insurance policy, you're probably wise to consider a quality mutual fund—or a single GIC—rather than trying to split it five ways into GICs with different maturities.

Of course, if you receive a large sum of money and you feel you don't have the investment skills to manage it yourself, you could consider hiring a professional money manager, who can be given the discretion to manage your investments, after establishing your investment objectives with you. Fees for this kind of service would be a percentage of the assets in the portfolio. The percentage varies with the size of the portfolio. But most money managers will not accept a portfolio under a certain amount, which is often as much as $1 million, but can be as low as $150,000 in some cases. If you're looking for this kind of professional assistance, the advice is still to ask around and try to find someone who has used this kind of service and is happy with the results. You may also want to set up appointments with several different individuals so you can form a personal impression of their approach to money management and investing. If you're going to pay a professional to manage your money, it's essential that you're confident in that person's ability to do so. You can only decide that if you speak to that individual personally.

Turning a Home into a Pension

Regardless of what you may have been able to save for retirement, whether in your RRSP, or through other savings or investments, if you own a home, you may have another source of income in retirement—particularly if the home is mortgage-free. Financial advisers generally suggest that investing in your own home is a very good way of saving for retirement. It may even be as important as saving money or contributing to your RRSP. If you are able to buy a home when you're younger and pay off the mortgage over the years, you will have "rent-free" accommodation in your old age. As mentioned earlier, some estimates put the value of a mortgage-free home at as much as 20 percent of your pre-retirement income, a figure to keep in mind when you're thinking of how to meet your income-replacement goals. In other words, following the earlier rule of thumb that your retirement income needs to be about 70 percent of your pre-retirement income to maintain your standard of living, if you have a mortgage-free home, you would need only 50 percent of your pre-retirement income to keep up with what you had coming in before retirement.

Personally, I'd say those estimates are probably too generous. For one thing, even though your mortgage is paid off, you will still have to pay for the maintenance and upkeep of your property. You'll still have property taxes, and maybe condominium fees, not to mention heating, hydro, repairs, and all the other expenses that are not going to go away just because your mortgage is paid off. The other thing to keep in mind is that reaching the point when your mortgage is paid off will not necessarily coincide with your retirement date. If you bought your home in your twenties, you may have finished paying off your mortgage by the time you were in your fifties. Consequently, if you retire in your sixties, your household expenses are not going to suddenly drop.

However, there is one situation where paying off your mortgage can give a boost to your retirement income. That's if, when you no longer have to make your monthly mortgage payments, you allocate the same amount of money to your retirement fund instead—a strategy I highly recommend. When you finally retire—whatever definition you choose to give that term—you will no longer need to make the monthly payments. You will be able to start drawing on your retirement income instead.

Regardless of your careful preparations for retirement, if your workplace pension is not indexed for inflation, or your RRSP has been invested in interest-bearing GICs, you may eventually be hit by increased rates of inflation, or even falling interest rates—as many of today's seniors have been. These people had counted on interest income to supplement what may have been a less-than-generous pension. If you get a few years into retirement and you realize your planned retirement income isn't going to be enough to support yourself, you may want to consider how you could tap into the equity you have built up in your home to add to your other retirement income.

There are ways in which owning a mortgage-free home may provide you with a source of extra cash, if you feel you don't have enough pension income from other sources. For example, you may want to consider trading down to a smaller home when you retire. By selling your current home and buying a smaller or less expensive one, you can free up additional funds that you can invest to supplement your pension income. This option is becoming increasingly popular with older Canadians, many of whom like to sell an expensive city home and move to the country cottage, or buy a home in a smaller town, where house prices and the cost of living may be lower.

Canada's current tax structure favours this type of arrangement, because any capital gain you make when you sell your principal residence is tax-free. That's why paying off your mortgage over your lifetime can be looked on as a form of long-term forced saving for retirement.

But one note of caution if you want to consider the "trading down" option. Choose your timing carefully. David Foot, whose 1996 book, *Boom, Bust and Echo,* chronicles the powerful influence of demographics on the economy, warns that if you're a member of the baby boom generation—that is, if you were born between 1947 and 1966—trading down could be a problem, because everyone your age may have the same idea at the same time. Foot suggests that, because baby boomers will all be trying to sell their city homes at the same time, prices of city homes will drop, making it difficult to realize the kind of proceeds you may have hoped for. And because these people will all be trying to buy cheaper homes in small towns at the same time, the prices of these homes will rise, frustrating the intention of this huge generation of Canadians to trade down their homes and free up extra cash for retirement.

Again, planning ahead may help you avoid this situation. For example, if you hope to move to the country eventually, you may be able to purchase a smaller home outside the city now, and renovate and perhaps expand it gradually over the years. When the time comes to sell your city home, you will already have bought and paid for your home in the country, and the proceeds of selling your current home can be used to supplement your pension. Because you will be selling your principal residence, any capital gain you make when you sell will be tax-free.

Reverse Mortgages

But many seniors don't want to sell their homes. If you've lived in the same community for many years, you may not want to uproot yourself and move to a different place, leaving your friends and neighbours, and all your familiar haunts. Depending on what part of the country you live in, you may be able to tap into your home for funds, without moving to a new location. In Ontario and British Columbia, you may be able to make arrangements for a "reverse mortgage"—or, more accurately, a "reverse annuity mortgage"—which will give you regular annuity payments for the rest of your life, using your home as collateral.

It's called a "reverse" mortgage, because, although your home is mortgaged, instead of making monthly mortgage payments, you receive a regular monthly income. It sounds too good to be true and, indeed, there are some drawbacks. As well, many people, having finally managed to pay off the mortgage on their home, are reluctant to go into debt by taking out another mortgage. But if you need additional income in retirement, you may want to look into this option. Here's how it works.

You find a lender who will give you a lump-sum payment, which is tax-free, or a lifetime annuity, based on the value of your home. The annuity gives you monthly payments for life and the income is also tax-free. As with any other annuity (see Chapter 5), you can choose a guarantee period, but the longer the guarantee, the lower the monthly payment you'll get. In the meantime, the lender holds a mortgage on the house, but you don't have to make any mortgage payments. The amount you owe is registered on the property title, but legally you still own your home. That means you can rent it out, or even sell it, but the mortgage debt must be paid off if you sell. In any case, it must be paid off when you die.

If you decide a reverse mortgage is for you, your home will have to be appraised, and the amount the lender is willing to provide will be based on a percentage of the appraised value. You won't be able to get a reverse mortgage for the full value of your home. The amount you can borrow under these arrangements varies from 15 to

42 percent of the appraised value of the house. The average is about 27 percent of the appraised value, and the average mortgage is about $75,000. The older you are, the more you'll likely be able to borrow, because the less time there is for the value of your home to drop below the amount of your indebtedness, leaving the lender holding the bag. Of course, house prices may also increase. But if your home increases in value after you have set up the reverse mortgage arrangement, there will be no detrimental impact on the lender. At present, reverse mortgages are available only to those individuals above the age of 62.

Because no payments are made on the mortgage, the debt mounts very quickly, which is a major problem with the arrangement. Your debt may double within 10 years. In fact, the outstanding debt can increase much faster than the value of your house, leaving you with very little capital if you decide to sell. That's why the reverse mortgage concept is probably better suited to those who plan to live in the house for the rest of their lives. One financial planner gives the example of a couple whose home is worth $500,000, where the husband is 72 and the wife is 70, who might take a reverse mortgage of $177,700. This provides them with a monthly income of $1,342.28. They also get a lump-sum payment of $1,500, with which they can pay the charges involved to set up the arrangement. But suppose the mortgage rate is 10.8 percent. In five years, the couple will owe $300,672. However, if the house has been appreciating in value by 3 percent a year, it will then be worth almost $580,000—more than enough to pay off the debt at that point.

What if the house does not increase in value, so that the outstanding debt when you die—or if you want to sell the house before then—is more than the house is worth? In this case, you are protected because the reverse mortgage agreement states that if the sale of the home won't pay off the mortgage entirely, the lender will not go after any other assets to satisfy the debt. In fact, that's the key to why a reverse mortgage is generally set at such a low percentage of the value of the home, namely, by setting it low the lender avoids a situation where the value of the home drops below the homeowner's outstanding debt. But that may be cold comfort if you want to sell the home at some point and are faced with a huge debt to pay.

Rates of interest on a reverse mortgage are fixed at about 1 percentage point above the rate for a conventional mortgage and reviewed every five years. The rate of interest paid on the lump sum used to buy the annuity is about 2 to 3 percentage points below the rate charged on the mortgage. Because the cost of borrowing can be used to offset the interest earned on the annuity for tax purposes, the annuity income is tax-free.

If you like the idea of a reverse mortgage, you should know that you can't just drop in at your local bank or trust company and get one. At the time of writing, the only place in Canada you can get a reverse mortgage is through Canadian Home Income Plan™ Corporation (CHIP™), a private company based originally in Vancouver. No major financial institution in Canada offers reverse annuity mortgages, although the Toronto-Dominion Bank expressed an interest in them in late 1995 by agreeing to refer clients in Ontario and British Columbia to CHIP™. TD Bank does not yet provide funding for the CHIP™ reverse mortgages, but the bank said it may eventually set up its own reverse mortgage program. Other banks have apparently also expressed an interest in being associated with the CHIP™ program. You can get more information by writing to Canadian Home Income Plan™ Corporation, #1108 – 30 St. Clair Avenue West, Toronto, Ontario M4V 3A1.

While other financial institutions may have products they call "reverse mortgages," these are actually short-term loans, which allow you to borrow money using your home as collateral, without making any loan payments for a few years. The intention of these loans is to help people who have a temporary cash shortage—for example, those who would like to take a few years off to travel. At one trust company, a mortgage loan, amortized over 25 years and for not more than 50 percent of the appraised value of the home, may be used to buy an annuity for a five-year term. At the end of that time, the annuity income ceases, but the mortgage payments begin and continue until the debt is paid off. Under these arrangements, your debt will compound, just as it would with a reverse annuity mortgage, but the arrangement is not intended to provide you with a regular income for the rest of your life, as a reverse annuity mortgage can.

Be sure you understand all the ins and outs of the arrangement before you get into a reverse annuity mortgage that offers you income for the rest of your life. For example, if you really want to leave your home to your children when you die, this arrangement is not for you. Nor is it appropriate if you think you may want to sell your home at some point in the future. In fact, you'll find that if you decide to go with a reverse mortgage, you will be required to seek independent legal advice, and to provide a certificate saying you've done so.

Reverse mortgages have been slow to catch on in Canada. A survey done for Canada Mortgage and Housing a few years ago, for example, indicated that 79 percent of those surveyed were not interested in reverse annuity mortgages, and only 4 percent were very interested in them. But reverse mortgages have proved popular in other countries. In the United Kingdom, for instance, a number of building societies—similar to our trust companies—offer them. But U.K. tax laws make the arrangement attractive. Homeowners there can reduce the value of their estate by leaving the reverse mortgage debt unpaid. That means less inheritance tax to pay when the homeowner dies. Canada doesn't have inheritance taxes—at least, not yet. Apart from not wanting to get into debt again so soon after getting out of it, many seniors in Canada seem to want to leave the family home to the children. With a reverse mortgage, the debt owing to the financial institution must be paid off when the homeowner dies.

Financial planners warn that a reverse mortgage is definitely not for everyone. Generally speaking, the older you are, the better a reverse mortgage works. In fact, some planners suggest these arrangements are most appropriate for people above the age of 70. You should also consider carefully how badly you need the money and how important it is for you to leave the full value of your home to your children (or to your estate). There's no doubt that this is an expensive way to get additional money. But, in some circumstances, a reverse mortgage can be a lifesaver. One financial planner gives the example of a client whose husband died, who had no children to inherit the house, and whose mortgage payments were just too much for her. Her existing mortgage was replaced with a reverse mortgage, which was ideal for her under the circumstances.

It's possible that the major financial institutions will show more interest in reverse annuity mortgages as Canada's population ages and more and more people want to tap into the value of their homes to provide additional retirement income for themselves. In fact, according to some predictions, reverse annuity mortgages will be widely available within the next five to ten years, but that may depend on how the housing market fares. Major lenders entering the field will need to feel some assurance that the home on which they've lent money will maintain its value. Otherwise, lenders could be faced with being unable to collect the homeowner's outstanding debt because the value of the home has dropped below the amount still owed. In some cities, home values have been dropping recently, which does not augur well for the future availability of reverse mortgages in all parts of Canada.

Reverse mortgages might also become more widely available if Canada's tax policy changes—for example, if capital gains on your principal residence were ever to be subject to tax, or if Canada introduced an estate tax, which would tax the value of assets handed on to the next generation when a person dies, as most other industrialized countries, including the United States, do. So stay tuned. By the time you get to retirement, reverse mortgages may be the hottest financial product around. In the meantime, if you need additional money to add to your pension income, you may find that the easier route to tapping into the equity in your home is to trade down to a less expensive model.

CHAPTER 9

WORKING TOWARD YOUR FUTURE FINANCIAL SECURITY

Throughout this book, discussion has focused on strategies you might use to accumulate funds for your senior years. If you're still young, you have plenty of time to get together the kind of money you need to establish your future financial security. If you're in your late forties or even older and you're only just starting to think seriously about planning for retirement, you're clearly facing quite a challenge. One thing that may help, though, is to try to be flexible in thinking about retirement. You'll only make it more difficult for yourself if you have a fixed idea of stopping your paid employment completely, once you get to a particular age. You may just be setting yourself up for a lot of worry and stress, and end up disappointed.

Your Retirement Transition

It may be much more productive, and certainly less stressful, to think about your retirement as a process, rather than an arbitrary fixed point in time. Consider it a time in your life when you'll be going through a change of pace. As mentioned before, the labour market of the 1990s is very different from the kind of labour market Canada had in the 1970s or even the 1980s. More and more employers are looking for a "just-in-time" work force to match their "just-in-time" production. They're less and less interested in long-term, permanent employees. Increasingly, they're contracting out work, hiring temporary and part-time workers, or getting the people they need through employment agencies that supply these kinds of workers.

About 40 percent of all women's jobs in Canada are now this kind of work, so you may already be working in one of these "non-standard" jobs. Perhaps you're doing contract work or working part-time. You may have a temporary or part-year job, or perhaps you're self-employed. These kinds of jobs rarely have any kind of pension protection. And because your work is probably unstable and may not be very well paid, it may be harder for you to save for retirement. For financial reasons, if nothing else, you may want to continue working after the "normal" retirement age of 60 or 65. But that's not necessarily all bad. It could be that you like the kind of work you're doing, and as long as you still feel up to it, there's no reason why you can't continue to do it, without having to stop once you reach a particular age. It may also be possible to scale back the hours you work as you get older, so that you have more leisure time, but you still have an income coming in to supplement what you will get from the CPP and perhaps from your own RRSP savings.

If you're working in a more traditional kind of job—what economists call a "standard" job—you may want to think about retirement as the time in your life when you'll be shifting gears. You may or may not get a workplace pension from your current employer. But even if you have to leave that job by the time you're 65, you can still expect to live another 20 years, on average, beyond that. You might begin your process of transition by taking early retirement from your current job—say at 55—and easing into something else.

Perhaps you've always wanted to go into business for yourself. If so, a key part of planning for the future should be figuring out what kind of business would work for you and how to save the start-up funds you'll need. That can be part of your planned saving goal too.

Perhaps you have a hobby that can be turned into a money-making venture as you get closer to your fifties or sixties. Now's the time to be thinking about that and planning how to achieve your goal. Perhaps you'd like to go into a different line of work that will give you a bit more time to yourself. Planning ahead for that should be part of your retirement plan, too. You might take appropriate courses or training so that you'll be ready when the time comes. You may just want to slow down the pace of your life as you get older, by moving from a full-time job in a particular industry to a part-time job in some other line of work.

There are already signs that Canadians are starting to see retirement in this new light. In fact, if you want a glimpse of what retirement will look like in the early years of the next century, you can see it in a fall 1996 publication from Statistics Canada called *Canada's Changing Retirement Patterns*. The book is based on findings from the 1994 General Social Survey—a survey that regularly gathers data on the demographic and social characteristics of Canadians. In line with the preference that many Canadians seem to have for early retirement, the survey showed the average retirement age for women was 58.5 years and 61.4 for men.

Perhaps the most intriguing finding of the 1994 survey was that 13 percent of retirees reported they had returned to paid work following their initial retirement. StatsCan couldn't really compare this number with earlier surveys because of differences in measurement methods. But it noted that "this phenomenon is also present in the United States and appears to be growing."

Even more interesting was the finding that of those retirees who reported returning to the work force, only 25 percent cited financial reasons. Twenty percent reported that they went back to work because they wanted something to occupy their free time; another 20 percent cited personal preference; and 35 percent gave other reasons. Most of those who went back to work took part-time jobs, although most of them had been working full-time before they retired. Of those who went back to work, 33 percent were self-employed, which was a much higher percentage than the percentage of people who reported they were self-employed before retirement. Temporary and contract work also accounted for significant percentages of those who returned to work after retirement. Here is "retirement as a transition" in action, and more and more people are experiencing it.

Some of these trends may be helped along by the changes now being considered for the Canada Pension Plan. As discussed earlier, one option on the table, for example, is raising the age of eligibility for a full CPP pension from 65 to 67 years. Some people are advocating raising it to the age of 70, although there doesn't seem to be much public support for that. The proposal for a partial pension seems much more interesting for the work force of the twenty-first century. We may see this proposal given serious consideration over the next decade or so.

As government pension programs are cut back, and private retirement savings prove inadequate, financial considerations will force many people to go on working. But, given the trends that now seem to be emerging, you may find your decision about continuing to work will be influenced even more by that need to occupy your time in some meaningful way. More and more Canadians seem to be coming to that conclusion.

The other key thing to keep in mind is the way public policy on pensions and retirement incomes is now developing. As governments cut back their spending and as public support for social insurance programs seems to be weakening, there's no doubt that the emphasis of retirement incomes policy will be to shift much more of the risk and the responsibility of providing for retirement onto individuals. Increasingly, Canadians will be on their own when it comes to providing for their future financial security. Old Age Security, with its once universal benefit, will soon be gone. In its place, we'll see an income-tested Seniors Benefit, with benefits given only to those whose income is below a certain threshold, and where the income test is based on family income. Canada Pension Plan benefits will almost certainly be cut—if not directly, then in ways such as a cap on indexing or limits on surviving-spouse benefits and drop-out periods, which will have the same impact. In this kind of political climate, it will be even more important to get your finances under control and plan carefully for the future.

The Key Pointers

Summarizing everything that has been discussed in this book, here are some key pointers for you.

- Regardless of how old you are, start now to think about planning for a secure financial future for yourself.
- Recognize that, because you are a woman, you have different retirement planning needs than a man does. You probably earn less, you may retire earlier, and you'll likely live longer. And if you're married or in a relationship, or if you ever were in the past, your family responsibilities will no doubt have a marked—and maybe even permanent—impact on your earnings and your ability to save for retirement. (The impact may be positive or negative.)
- Try to be realistic about the expectations you have for your retirement—however you choose to define that term. Make sure your plans are based on adequate information that is as accurate as you can make it.
- Think about when you may want to make your retirement transition, and don't be fixated on an arbitrary retirement age.
- Make sure you take your family situation into account, planning the transition with your spouse or partner, if you have one, and

thinking about other family members for whom you may have to be responsible as you enter your senior years.

- Consider carefully the age at which you'll become eligible for various sources of retirement income including government benefits, your workplace pension (if you have one), and the income from your RRSP. And find out if you will be subject to mandatory retirement under your workplace pension plan.
- Start thinking about how you'd like to spend your senior years and how much money you'd need to do the kind of things you'd like to do.
- Do a tally of how much you've already saved toward your goals, how much you'll be entitled to get from various government programs and your workplace pension, and how much more you need to save each year to meet your objectives, using the worksheets in Chapter 3.
- Be prepared to adjust your goals if you come up with an impossible annual savings target. Consider how you might phase into other kinds of work that would give you more leisure time but continue to provide you with some retirement income to supplement what you expect to get from other sources.
- Consider getting some help to do the calculations if you find your situation is too complex, or you're not sure you can do it on your own.

Government Programs

- Find out what you'll get from government programs when you reach retirement age. Remember, OAS and GIS may be gone by the time you're a senior. If you have a spouse or partner, you can't plan on getting anything from these programs because you probably don't know at this point what your joint income will be at age 65. (Even if you don't have a spouse or partner now, you could have one at age 65, which will affect your right to the new Seniors Benefit.)

- Check with the Income Security Programs office to find out how much you can expect from the CPP, assuming you continue to contribute and that the basic provisions of the plan won't change significantly. You can request a detailed calculation of your retirement benefit, based on your contributions so far, once every year.
- Watch carefully for changes to the Canada Pension Plan, which may be implemented in 1997. And check for any other changes that might be made before you get to the age of eligibility for CPP benefits. Find out if and how any of these changes might affect you.

Workplace Pension Plans

- If you haven't already done so, find out if you have a workplace pension plan and what kind of plan it is.
- If you received an employee booklet about the pension plan, read it carefully and ask your human resources department or your union to explain anything you don't understand.
- Find out what benefits your workplace pension plan will give you if you stay with your employer until you retire and what your options are if you don't.
- If you work part-time and you have the option to join the plan, try to take advantage of the option rather than taking cash in lieu of benefits.
- If you're in a same-sex relationship, find out if your workplace pension plan provides surviving-spouse benefits to your partner if you die.
- Check to see if your workplace pension plan is integrated with the CPP and what will happen if CPP benefits are reduced or the age of eligibility is increased. (You may have to ask your union representative about this.)
- If you have a defined contribution plan or a group RRSP and you get to choose how your fund is invested, work at acquiring the expertise you need to make good investment decisions. Take

courses, go to seminars, read financial books and newspapers, and try to improve your self-confidence as an investor.

- Take advantage of your right to information about your workplace pension plan. If what you're given is written in incomprehensible jargon, ask for an explanation.

RRSPs

- If you're entitled to contribute to an RRSP, do it. And try to contribute the maximum you're allowed.
- Make your contribution early in the year so you can get the maximum benefit from tax-free compounding of the interest on your funds.
- Avoid making your RRSP contribution at the last minute when you don't have time to think about what you're doing.
- Try to contribute regularly every year.
- If you're a nervous or inexperienced investor, resolve to work on improving your knowledge and expertise, so you can get the best return, consistent with your objectives, on your RRSP investments.
- Consider quality mutual funds for your RRSP.
- Don't get into a self-directed RRSP unless you want more sophisticated types of investments and you're prepared to spend some time on it.
- If you can possibly avoid it, don't use your RRSP funds to buy a home, to pay for your maternity leave, or to support yourself if you lose your job. If you really can't avoid cashing in your plan for these reasons, try to make up for it by contributing an equivalent amount as quickly as possible. (If you borrow under the Home Buyers' Plan, you will have to pay back the funds, anyway.)

Counting on a Spouse or Partner

- If you have a spouse or partner, make sure you plan jointly for your financial future. Whether you have your own sources of income or not, you should know what sources of income you'll both have in retirement.

- If you don't have your own source of income or if you earn less than your partner, agree with your partner to earmark a regular monthly amount for you personally, so you can save and invest it for your retirement yourself.

Ongoing Relationships

- Find out about your mate's workplace pension plan (if there is one), his investments, RRSPs, and other financial assets. Know where they are held, what his funds are invested in, and what you would do if he died. Follow the same procedure if you have a same-sex partner.
- Find out what kinds of benefits your spouse or partner's workplace pension plan might provide when he retires.
- Consider whether it's worthwhile to share your joint CPP pension credits with your spouse or common-law partner when you both reach retirement age.
- Get your spouse or common-law partner to contribute to an RRSP in your name if you don't have earned income of your own.
- Make sure you know how much money is in your spousal RRSP and how it is invested. Play an active role in investing your funds—the plan belongs to you, even if your spouse makes the contributions.

Divorce or the End of a Relationship

- Be sure to notify the CPP if you get divorced, so you can share the CPP credits built up during your marriage. Remember, if you're legally separated or in a common-law relationship, you must apply for credit-splitting when your relationship ends and there are time limits for doing so.
- Find out if provincial or federal laws provide for you to share your spouse's workplace pension if your marriage or relationship ends.

Make sure you get good professional advice if your family assets include a workplace pension that must be valued.

Widowhood

- If you're a low-income widow, aged 60 to 64, check with the Income Security Programs office to see if you're eligible for a Spouse's Allowance benefit.
- Make sure you know what surviving-spouse pension you may be entitled to get from the CPP on your spouse's death, and be aware that it depends on your age and on whether or not you have dependents.
- Don't sign away your right to a surviving-spouse pension from his workplace pension unless other arrangements have been made for your financial support in the event of his death.
- Make sure you know what benefits his workplace pension will pay out if he dies before retirement. If you receive a lump-sum payment from his workplace pension plan, try to roll it over into your RRSP.
- Be aware that his RRSPs or RRIFs can be rolled over to you without tax consequences if he dies.
- Find out what life insurance coverage your spouse or partner has and make sure you are named as beneficiary.

Other Ways of Providing a Retirement Income

- If you are married or in a relationship, learn to assert yourself financially.
- If you don't work outside the home, build up your own retirement fund one step at a time with money you receive as gifts, inheritances, and even the proceeds of garage sales.
- Add to your retirement nest egg by careful investment of lump-sum settlements you may receive as a result of divorce or widowhood.

- If you own a home, be aware that you can turn it into extra retirement income by trading down to a less expensive home and investing the difference.
- Investigate a reverse mortgage if you think you won't have enough income in retirement.

Strategies to Help You Save

Saving for the future is never easy, especially when you may have other priorities, such as buying a home or paying for the kids' education. One tried and true method is to "pay yourself first." Once you've done your calculations and have decided how much you want to save each month, take that amount off the top. The best and most painless way to do it is to arrange for a pre-authorized debit to your bank, trust company, or credit union account. The money can be directed to your RRSP with the same institution or to a mutual fund. If the money comes out of your account automatically, you don't have to decide each month how much you're going to set aside. And you're not tempted to forego setting aside the money if something else comes up. This strategy also has the advantage that you are making regular deposits into your RRSP, instead of having to come up with a lump sum each year as the contribution deadline looms.

If you don't have earned income and are not entitled to contribute to an RRSP, try to allocate a regular monthly amount from your bank account to a mutual fund or special savings account. However small the amount, your savings will soon mount up.

If you're directing your monthly deposits into some kind of investment, such as a mutual fund or the purchase of stocks, you're doing what the experts call "dollar cost averaging." Because prices of stocks or mutual funds go up and down all the time, by investing a small amount each month, the cost of your investments will average out over time, which is preferable to what happens when you buy all your stocks in one month when the price may be high, or try to time your purchase when you think the price of the stock or the fund may have hit a low point.

Consider borrowing to invest, if the financial institution you deal with will lend you the money. The interest on money borrowed to invest is tax-deductible. You may also want to consider borrowing to invest in your RRSP. In this case, however, you will not be able to deduct the interest for tax purposes. But, because you'll get a tax deduction for the RRSP contribution, you can use your tax rebate to pay off a good chunk of the loan.

Above all, if you want to have a secure financial future, you need to start by being actively involved. If you know nothing about investing, find out. If you're intimidated by it, try to overcome your timidity by learning more about money management. The more knowledge you have, the more confident you'll be in handling your money. Above all, don't leave your financial future to chance and don't leave it in someone else's hands. It's up to you to plan for your own retirement; no one else can do it for you. But asserting your financial autonomy can be exhilarating and very rewarding. By taking charge yourself, you will have a much better chance of achieving the kind of future you want. Good luck!

INDEX